Praise for

"A must-read that goes beyond mere exit strategy to deal with an issue that's just as complex: the challenging emotions of ministry transition. Jeff's wisdom and honesty will prepare pastors to gracefully navigate leadership transitions, which is an area that seminary training often overlooks. A truly invaluable contribution to the limited field of transition literature!"

—Doug Schmidt
Senior Pastor,
Woodside Bible Church, SE Michigan

"There is no success without a successor. With playful metaphors and images, Jeff Harlow shares his personal journey of moving from successful lead pastor to successful transition for the new pastor of Crossroads Church. Dancing With Cinderella is a story of hope with signposts and principles for others to follow."

—Dave Travis
Chief Executive and Chief Encouragement Officer,
Leadership Network

"I found Dancing with Cinderella to be an incredibly well-written book and a must-read for any senior pastor thinking about passing the baton to a successor. In this book, Jeff offers a lot of practical tips from his own experiences on how to make what could be a difficult transition into a very natural and healthy process. It will certainly help me as I start to think about what it looks like to hand in my roll over to my successor."

—Steve Poe
Lead Pastor,
Northview Church, Carmel, IN

JEFF HARLOW

DANCING
—with—
CINDERELLA

LEADING A HEALTHY CHURCH TRANSITION

EPIPHANY
PUBLISHING

Library of Congress Control Number: 2017954719

ISBN 978-0986102813 (first edition, hard cover by Phaino Publishing)
ISBN 978-1946093035 (second edition, paperback)
ISBN 978-1946093042 (second edition, ebook)

This book was printed in the United States of America.
10 9 8 7 6 5 4 3 2 1

Epiphany Publishing
P.O. Box 36814
Indianapolis, IN 46236
www.epiphanypublishing.us
info@epiphanypublishing.us

CONTENTS

ACKNOWLEDGEMENTS

. . . .

"It's not good for a man to be alone." God said it early, and I'm a poster child of that fact. God taught me the value of teams long before I knew how desperately I needed them. I discovered that God had strategically placed key people alongside of me as certainly as He had designated a role for me in His plan.

I'm grateful to that small group of people that trusted me as a twenty-year-old to be its pastor. By God's design, I needed those people more than they needed me. Most of those dear people are in heaven now, but I hope those who remain know how precious they are to me.

Thanks to my staff and volunteer leaders who served so faithfully with me at Crossroads. I'm grateful God chose to invest them and their gifts in Crossroads. I'm particularly indebted to Kevin Smith and Carolyn Conner — both lifetime friends to Becky and me, and trusted personal assistants who filled in the gaps I created.

And to Chris Duncan — I've never regretted a second that God chose you to take the reins of Crossroads. Like a dad prays for a man to love his daughter and be the spiritual leader of their home, I prayed that God would find a pastor who would love Crossroads and be the spiritual leader in His plans. You are the answer to my prayers.

The writing of this book epitomizes my need for a team. I've always needed editors more than I wished, but for the editing of this book I'm extremely grateful to Lisa Fipps, Caroline Erickson, and Lee Warren. They brought lots of grit to the tumbling process of my writing.

Much of the joy of my journey has been connecting the dots of the people God put in my life. In addition to those already mentioned, I'd like to note my expression of gratitude for Kyle Parton and his team at Epiphany Publishing. It is a particular joy to have a dear friend's son, a Crossroads prodigy who evidenced God's favor throughout his childhood, and now the CEO of Epiphany, publish *Dancing with Cinderella*.

To my kids, Will, Leslie, Jessica, and Jennifer, I want to say how proud I am of you. Only you and God know the price you've paid in sharing your dad with so many, but you've never demonstrated it in how you've lived your life. You are raising wonderful families and serving the Lord as you do.

And to the one who has loved me most through it all — my bride, wife, and best mother and grandmother I know. You are my greatest asset. We were fifteen years old when God told you to "Be strong. You're going to be a pastor's wife." It was the same week He called me into the ministry. You came to realize God was prepping you because He knew you were going to be this pastor's wife. I've never cared what others thought until I found out what you believed. You are my partner in life and ministry. I love you, Becky.

PREFACE

. . . .

I always teased my pastor, Jeff Harlow, that I had seniority over him. I started attending Oakford Baptist Church when I was 1 week old. He didn't start preaching there until about seven years later. Quite frankly, I didn't want Jeff to be my pastor. He replaced the Rev. Albert Kimbler, who had led my dad to the Lord shortly before he died, which is when I was 13 months old. Since I never knew my dad, Albert held a special place in my heart for ensuring that my dad and I would spend eternity together. No one could be Albert. No one told me in advance that Albert was retiring and the elders had asked Jeff to be our new pastor. I felt sick to my stomach when I heard the announcement.

Oakford was a little white church with a steeple, the image found on classic Christmas cards. Lilac bushes lined the west side of the U-shaped gravel drive. After Jeff's first sermon, I walked out before the rest of my family and buried my head in the lilacs, hiding tears and praying God would bring Albert back. Where would my family be without Albert? What would happen to me?

The transition scared me. I was angry with Albert for leaving and didn't want to make Jeff feel welcome enough to stay. But Jeff has a way with people. He's funny, smart, and incredibly personable. He remembers everyone's name — everyone's. With less than 100 people attending

Oakford when he started his pastoral career, that was easy. As we built new facilities during the nearly four decades of his leadership and the average weekly attendance grew to 2,000, I'm sure it was difficult, but he did it. It's one of his gifts. He visited people's homes regularly. He got to know people, really know them. It wasn't until I visited other churches where pastors didn't know all the names of people who attended for years, let alone what their key life issues were, that I realized how special Jeff was.

One of my gifts is to pray for others. When I became one of Jeff's prayer partners, I had the privilege to hear Jeff's deepest heart cries to God. The Lord also revealed to me the tremendous burden Jeff carried for each and every person who had ever stepped foot in Oakford and Crossroads or ever would attend even just one service. I saw it as a huge boulder he carried day and night. Jeff never put down the boulder or complained about its heaviness. His repeated prayer was, "Please, Lord, help me reach them. Somehow, speak through me. Don't let me get in the way. Help me to say it right. Help them to hear. Help not one soul to be lost."

Over the years, Jeff wasn't just my pastor and prayer partner. He took on more titles in my life, most notably Friend and Father Figure. In the back of my mind, I knew the day would come that Jeff would retire. My heart couldn't imagine it though. When I heard the news, I felt sick to my stomach. No one could be Jeff.

Unlike the transition from Albert to Jeff, the church talked about the transition from Jeff to Pastor Chris Duncan a lot and from the start. Jeff made sure of that. It was a multi-step, multi-year transition. I can honestly say that if anyone could have been lost in transition, it would have been me. Everyone knows how much Jeff means to me.

As a writer and editor, Jeff asked me to review this book. I knew the story, but it wasn't until I was editing that I realized I was Cinderella. I am one of the many Cinderellas that Jeff mentions in this book with a name and a personal story.

I love that I am not only God's but also Crossroads' Cinderella. One of the too-many-to-count blessings God has given me in my life through Jeff's ministry is a smooth transition in the leadership of Crossroads. Your church is full of Cinderellas – people who are counting on you to get it right so we aren't led astray by false princes, weakened or frustrated in our faith, or wounded by feeling we don't matter enough for the outgoing and incoming leaders to take the time to consult God and to seek wise counsel from those like Jeff who know by God's instruction how to transition leadership.

The transition made it possible for me to know and be at peace with Jeff leaving. I knew in my spirit that God was Lord of the process, that retiring was the right move at the right time for Jeff, and that God placed Chris at the helm. I was able to say (albeit it through uncontrollable tears) to Jeff that his earthly and heavenly fathers were in heaven saying, "Well done my good and faithful servant," and to Chris, "Welcome to Crossroads."

— *Lisa Fipps*

INTRODUCTION

. . . .

Maybe you have the same unrest I had. I was haunted by the possibility that the ministry to which I had given my life might lose momentum and that the lights could dim after I was gone.

What happened at the church in Ephesus that dropped her from New Testament prominence to total extinction in a few decades? What happened in Albuquerque to my great-grandparents' church, once considered the most vibrant congregation in the Southwest, to reduce it to the musty smell of disuse in my lifetime? Could these churches have succumbed to the same mishandling of leadership transition that I watched destabilize three of the most prominent churches in my hometown as I began pastoring?

In more ways than one, the church is on the brink, and we cannot afford to stumble during the handoff to the next generation of leaders.

Our assignment as leaders is so strategic in God's plan that our mission must keep going after we cannot. The purposes to which the eternal God calls His church have longer shelf lives than the people He assigns to lead them.

Leadership transitions are so crucial that Jesus spent an additional forty days with His disciples after He finished His grueling mission on the cross to die for our sins. After spending thirty-three years on task on earth, three years teaching the crowds and training His disciples, all night and the next morning being beaten within an inch of His life, six hours on a cross suffering the most horrendous death ever endured, and three days in the grave breaking the chains of death, no one would have blamed Him to have not stopped ascending until He stepped across the threshold of the throne room.

That Jesus delayed His triumphal ascension after completing a list of that magnitude to ensure the readiness of His team to take His place ought to be more than a hint. If you think a leader is finished before his successor gets started, think again.

Small church or large church, old church or plant church, traditional church or contemporary church, obscure church or iconic church: an unhealthy leadership transition hurts people and cripples mission. Healthy leadership transition has always been crucial, but maybe never more than now as thousands of pastors who are leading the church growth era edge toward retirement or their next assignment.

God sensitized me early in my ministry to His own grief for the losses sustained when churches falter while transitioning from one leader to the next. I've written this book as a record of what He taught me during the leadership transition at Crossroads Community Church in Kokomo, Indiana, with Chris Duncan, my successor. Our churches simply do not have the margins in missional momentum, money and people to suffer a botched handoff.

This book is helpful to pastors who are thinking about their own inexorable transitions, as well as to church leadership, their respective boards, and the members of a church that is preparing for the exit of their current pastor and the entrance of their new leader.

Giving a daughter away on her wedding day, with all of its attending emotion, serves as a metaphor of the principles of leadership transition of a church. The courtship and marriage of Cinderella and Prince Charming provides the imagery of a church and her new leader as I share the transferable lessons God taught Crossroads and me while we navigated the waters of transition.

Dancing with Cinderella covers the principles of a healthy leadership transition in three parts: "Preparing for a Healthy Transition," "The Choreography of a Healthy Transition Plan," and "Living the New Day."

This book addresses many of the questions that a transition raises, such as:

- Why are transitions so difficult?
- What is really at the heart of the transition?
- How do a leader's objectives change after the transition starts?
- What happens with a God-idea when startup takes more time than a leader has left to finish it?
- How do departing leaders define future boundaries?
- What are the happy surprises of a healthy transition?

At the end of every chapter, you will find helpful questions that will prompt personal reflection and group discussion. I hope *Dancing with Cinderella* gives you more help than I had, as you take one of the biggest leadership steps of your tenure. You deserve the help, and the assignment demands it. I didn't intend for these steps to be formulaic, though they worked beautifully for Crossroads. Rather, the principles catalyze thoughts that can lead to a tailored strategy befitting of your unique culture and circumstances.

My highest hope is that you experience at the deepest level the fulfillment Jesus expressed when He said, "It is finished." How you leave, and with whom you leave Cinderella, will shape the future of the church or ministry you have led. It will cast the light by which you will evaluate the lasting impact of your labor of love. You can end well, and you will know it when you do.

PART 1

. . . .

PREPARING FOR

A HEALTHY TRANSITION

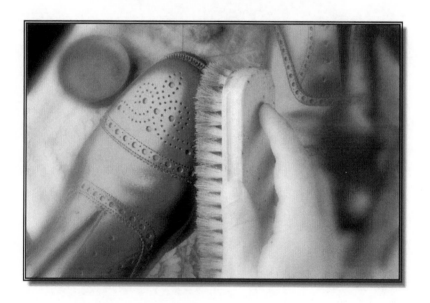

CHAPTER 1

THE DADDY-DAUGHTER DANCE

> *Great is the art of beginning,*
> *but greater the art of ending.*
>
> — HENRY WADSWORTH LONGFELLOW

Down deep, if you knew you gave your life to something much bigger than anything you could conceive in your own mind, wouldn't that realization be the most gratifying moment imaginable? Wouldn't you like to know that what you've worked for was really a God-thing entrusted to your leadership for a time? That what you've given everything to is so strategic in God's plan that it just has to keep going after you can't? Such a project would not only be worth leading in your generation, but it would be worth leaving in the hands of the next generation.

The need for transition never takes a visionary by surprise. How could a true visionary "get the picture" that only includes himself? When leaders only see a vision to the end of their involvement, it is short sided, if not sad. Leaders are supposed to lead good people with a worthy mission into the future, not let a movement die when they step away.

As surely as the daddy of a little girl discovers his princess has grown up and has set a wedding date to move on to the next stage of her life, sooner or later, a pastor becomes aware that his church is approaching a transition just as momentous. Not every little girl decides to become a bride, but 100 percent of thriving churches will move into the next season of ministry with another pastor or senior leader. The transition is not yours to stop, but it is yours to help facilitate.

Transitions, as God designed them, are unavoidable, but healthy ones aren't. You have to embrace transition as a strategic rite of passage. Since transitions are part of God's design, He surely has devised a way to do them right. We can settle for no less than exactly that.

WHY ARE TRANSITIONS SO DIFFICULT?

Giving a daughter away on her wedding day, with all of its attending emotion, serves as a metaphor of the leadership transition of a church. The courtship and marriage of Cinderella and Prince Charming provided the imagery of a church and her new leader as I journaled about the lessons God taught Crossroads and me while we navigated the waters of transition.

Both the giving of your daughter to the care of another man and the passing of the reins of your church into the hands of another leader are difficult to do. I know — they're not really ours. But we are parents, not babysitters; and shepherds, not hirelings — our heart connection to them certainly makes them feel like they are ours. You understand that neither of the two responsibilities were simply career assignments. They were rather an entrustment of the heavenly Father of both a little girl and a group of little believers the Bible says is becoming the Bride of Christ (Revelation 21:9). As the Father asked many of us as dads to raise little girls to a point of handoff, He has called leaders to play a strategic roll as a kind of bucket brigade to a final handover of a church to her true Groom, Jesus Christ.

Both a daughter and a church attach to your heart. You anticipate loving a daughter; loving your church may have come as a surprise. But either way, when attached at the heart, sharing it is difficult; yielding the primary leadership role in their lives is even more difficult.

But take heart. If a dad can make the transition on his daughter's wedding day, then a leader can make the transition for a church and her new Prince Charming. The emotions are so similar. It involves a lot more players, and demands careful strategy, as well as personal decisions that are challenging, but the principles are the same.

I am the dad of three daughters: Leslie, Jessica, and Jennifer. I was also the pastor of Crossroads Community Church in Kokomo, Indiana, for nearly thirty-eight years. The transition to another man started with each daughter after she reached her twenties, and her engagement usually lasted about a year. The transition of my church to another senior leader started after thirty-four years and that engagement lasted over three years.

Those three girls, as well as my church, were the catalysts to four of the most instantaneous and momentous transitions of my life. Though the process was subtle, the moment of handoff was conspicuous. It's a moment you can miss: So don't.

A HEALTHY TRANSITION IS LIKE A WELL-CHOREOGRAPHED DANCE

Common sense and life experience go a long way in figuring out the steps in a transition. But make no mistake; you have to choreograph the dance of a healthy transition. Crossroads, Chris Duncan (my successor), and I took definable steps that do not need to be mimicked, but you must cover the same dance floor with strategic steps that flow out of the principles of a healthy transition. I hope to offer you more help than I had.

You don't need me to say much about the first thirty-four years I pastored Crossroads, but certain details of the last three and a half years might be of some help if the same Holy Spirit who asked you to lead your church is now hinting that your role is nearly complete and He has another mentor in mind. I do not intend to hand you a formula, but I do believe you should consider the principles I'm about to offer and then develop a plan to individualize your steps.

A healthy transition process should unfold in such a manner that, both in planning and real time, progress can be plotted on a continuum. Both ends are easy to plot. Only the feel and flow of everything that comes between is in question. I want to help you understand that the more attention you give to those points between the beginning and the end, the more the handoff will be successful.

The privilege of ending my tenure on the highest notes of my ministry by every measure was a blessing. At the time of the writing of this book, the church has logged its first year beyond me, under the leadership of Chris. I am thrilled to tell you that Crossroads has made progress up the crescendo of successful mission since I took my seat as a supportive well-wisher. More people are attending now than in my day. Giving has increased by fourteen percent in that same period. The church is moving forward with the same mission, based on the same values, and with evolving strategies. It's like watching your kids flourish after they leave your home to begin their own lives.

DON'T TRIP ON YOUR SWAN SONG

As good as I feel about the entire transition process as a pastor, I can't believe I almost missed one of the biggest father-daughter moments as a dad. My oldest daughter, Leslie, had finalized all but one of the last elements of the wedding as only an engineer's personality could detail it. She still needed to secure her dad for that once-in-a-lifetime dance at the reception.

I want to believe I was just kidding when I told her no, but there is some evidence to convict me on the charge that I wasn't. Leslie thinks I tried to blame it on my Baptist roots and senior pastor position. My argument must have been better than that!

I do admit to not being comfortable with the idea. Though I had an older, cooler cousin who taught me the waltz progressive step as a kid, that had been thirty-something years earlier; and I had never been light on my feet when on the dance floor. Plus, I had not danced since high school. Maybe I wasn't kidding.

The most incriminating evidence is the future son-in-law to father-in-law talk that ensued between the "Big Ask" to a daddy-daughter dance, and the "Big Day" when my princess and her prince would get married. I remember Curt, Leslie's prince, losing any semblance of intimidation while looking me in the eye during our private conversation and saying, "This is a once-in-a-lifetime moment with your daughter. You will break her heart if you say no. So, don't."

Thankfully, Curt helped me get our dance off on the right foot by convincing me to say yes. Leslie and I did practice the night before (with no one watching), and pulled it off without a hitch during the big moment (when everyone was watching). A photo captured the moment etched for a lifetime in my heart: my little girl dancing in her daddy's arms.

The first time I heard Steven Curtis Chapman sing his song, "Cinderella," I couldn't help but think about walking all three of my daughters down an aisle toward their respective Prince Charmings. I had messed up plenty of days before then, but not their wedding days. I danced with my Cinderellas.

As you think about the future of your church, you simply can't afford to trip on your swan song, shaking the confidence and losing the momentum of her new song as she dances into the future of God's plans for her.

THE STAGGERING COST OF A FAILED TRANSITION

As unsettling as it is, you would be wise to take the time to calculate the cost of a bungled transition. As one young chair of a church finance committee was heard to say, "Nothing educates like an invoice."

At stake is your church's dowry, which is instrumental to the success of her future. It may reek of business to you, but the stability of your church's finances, leadership team, and membership roll is mission critical. You are as accountable for the guardianship of their transfer as you were of their stewardship during your administration.

THE LOSS OF PEOPLE

You can cry foul and attempt to guilt people with calls for loyalty, but unhealthy transitions can lead to unhealthy environments, and unhealthy environments lead to empty seats. When that happens, it isn't a foul. It's the result of instability. I believe that at the heart of the church's mission is people, and watching them walk away because a church has become unstable and unhealthy is the hardest loss of all from which to recover.

THE EROSION OF RESOURCES

Empty seats lead to reduced giving. Reduced giving leads to reduced programming. Reduced programming leads to exiting staff. And all of the above leads to more empty seats, which accelerates the downward spiral.

THE POLARIZATION OF EMOTIONAL DISTRESS

Some costs are less tangible, but equally undeniable. The emotional costs stemming from unhealthy transitions are impossible to quantify, but easy to qualify. Solomon described it candidly, "An offended friend is harder to win back than a fortified city. Arguments separate friends like a gate locked with bars" (Proverbs 18:19, NLT). Unity in the church is priceless, as it generates synergy. Emotional distress is debilitating, as it provokes relational breakdown. If you've experienced polarization in the church due to unhealthy leadership transitions, you know exactly the pain of which I speak and the toll it takes.

THE EBB OF MOMENTUM

Lost momentum from unhealthy transitions threatens the success of the mission. John Maxwell calls momentum the leader's best friend. Having it and losing it is one of the most gut-wrenching realities I've endured as a leader. It is a precious commodity in the life of a congregation. It makes everything seem doable, and easier. The pain that comes with emotional distress turns all energy inward and kills momentum. Lost momentum diverts energy from missional programming; the church goes from strategic thinking to managing crises.

THE DECLINE OF MORALE

Diminished morale is similar, but not synonymous with lost momentum. They are inextricably linked, but morale lies at the heart of momentum. When the confidence and enthusiasm of high morale wanes, risk taking and sacrifice for the mission declines, and with them the wins that create momentum. It is a vicious cycle that demonstrates Maxwell's Law of the Big Mo: Momentum is easier to steer than start.

Those are the tolls exacted on churches left vulnerable to unplanned, unhealthy transitions. Those are catastrophic losses that can never be explained to the Great Shepherd. The costs are too great to ignore.

GOD'S PURPOSES HAVE LONGER SHELF LIVES THAN HIS LEADERS

You've probably heard the saying that there are three ways to leave a leadership position of a church: get carried out, get escorted out, or walk out on your own terms. Having my first step in heaven directly preceding my last step in ministry on earth would be a cool way to leave, but that's generally more storybook than textbook. God allowed my wife, Becky, and me to walk out on our own terms.

The purposes to which the eternal God calls His church have longer shelf lives than the people who He assigns to lead them. In addition, He wants no confusion in the minds of His people as to the value of the vision. He also wants to make it clear who the real leader always has been and always will be. Healthy transitions demonstrate both of those absolutes.

If healthy leadership transition really is that vital, why do we miss it so often and so easily? I'm afraid we get careless; or of all the ironies, we live in denial. Both are unacceptable by our own standards.

Father God set the precedent a long time ago. He assigns others to pick up what He asks you to lay down. He finished the Exodus without Moses, leading His people into Canaan with Joshua. He continued to build a nation beyond the exploits of David and used Solomon to take Israel to another level of renown. He even answered the prayer of His Son to extend the rule of His Kingdom on earth through people after Jesus returned to heaven.

He cast the die, and His ways are set. Someone is waiting in the wings to continue what you've been doing after you're gone. It's not a matter of if, but *when*. Thank God He has engaged you in something that's too important to fade after you do.

It is understandable if you question what seems to be a presupposition on my part that all churches, once they have begun, are supposed to continue forever. Circumstances shift and seasons change that make it understandable for Jesus to decide to close the book and not just a chapter on the purposes of a church. My challenge to you is to let Him decide if it's time for a church to put the last period to its story. Don't become the catalyst to a premature end because you bungled the transition to your successor.

The role of leadership is mission critical to the success of any purpose. That, too, is part of God's grand design, supported by the evidence of His provision of the gift of leadership, and the attending directive in Romans 12:8 to lead with diligence. The axiom, you are where you've been led, is an observation on our part, but the design was on His part.

Every healthy church is comprised of its multiple ministries and subgroups. Though I'm writing as a former senior pastor, the critical nature of the subject is germane to the continuity of any age appropriate or need-based ministry and its purpose within the scope of a church or parachurch ministry. If a ministry is successful, it has leadership. If it has leadership, then its long-term success is incumbent on healthy transitions to the next generation of growth and experience.

DON'T FOLLOW THESE EXAMPLES

When did you come to understand that you or someone else could bungle the transition? Do you remember thinking, *They messed that transition up big time*? Take the time to pay attention to their inattention.

Paul told the Corinthians that part of the purpose of Scripture is for us to learn from the tragic mistakes of others. He writes, "These things happened to them as examples and were written down as warnings for us, on whom the culmination of the ages has come" (1 Corinthians 10:11).

The Lord drilled the possibility of fouled up transitions into my soul early in ministry. I watched three churches with strong leaders when I was a young pastor. The pastors were great examples of how to build an effective ministry. But when it came to their transition to another stage of their own lives, the evidence indicates they messed up the daddy-daughter dance with their church. Each of the churches they led, at best, lost momentum after they were gone. All three ministries diminished to a shadow of their original scale. As I watched their churches struggle after their departure, I sensed the Holy Spirit clarify that He had directed my attention to their ministries, not just to learn how to lead, but *how not to leave*.

I couldn't bear to think of the church I loved, and the vision to which I was giving the best years of my life, falling into declivity. I knew God didn't want that. I vowed it would never happen under my watch.

I wish I could tell you my track record in this pursuit of finding Prince Charming was perfect. I've played the role of Samuel at Jesse's house on more than one occasion. I've gone through Jesse's sons knowing the next king was in sight, only to have the Lord keep me from making a mistake He couldn't afford. I believe God was gracious to me in those near misses because my motives were pure, but He wasn't going to let my pure intentions mess up His master plans. He stopped me as cold in my tracks as He did Samuel. But Samuel didn't get discouraged with God's, "Are you kidding me?" When it looked like he was at the end of the line, he had the common sense to assume the line continued out of sight. Sure enough, the next king came from a sheep pasture. David was worth the wait.

We'll talk about finding the next you in a later chapter. For now, all we need to settle is that he's out there. And out of sight can't afford to be out of mind.

If you're a dad with a daughter, practice your dancing. If you're the senior leader of the bride of Christ, get your dancing shoes ready.

TIME TO REFLECT

. . . .

1) What condition would you like your church to be in when the leadership transition starts?

2) What issues do you need to address before the church enters a leadership transition?

3) Make a list of churches or component ministries that have struggled because of an unhealthy leadership transition.

4) Spend time thinking through the impact of a poor transition in your church. What are your areas of risk? What would be the impact of losing 10 percent of your congregation? Which areas of your church would a 10 percent reduction in financial resources impact?

5) Who could you imagine God using to mentor you through the timing and strategies of your leadership transition?

CHAPTER 2

· · · · · · · · · · · · · · · ·

RECALIBRATING YOUR REALITY

> *Instead of seeing the rug being pulled from under us, we can learn to dance on a shifting carpet.*
>
> – THOMAS CRUM

Am I alone, or do you catch yourself at the oddest times realizing that status quo isn't so static? Could that airport conveyor sense of movement when you're not even walking be due to living the reality about which Solomon wrote? In his twilight years, he caught himself reflecting, "He has made everything beautiful in its time. He has also set eternity in the hearts of men; yet they cannot fathom what God has done from beginning to end" (Ecclesiastes 3:11).

If we slow down for just a moment as we drive our rutted roads on typical days we might well catch that sense of the eternal in our soul. It doesn't cast a shadow on the beauty of what is occupying our time in the moment, but it does whisper that *there's something more beyond now.* Could it be that, although God doesn't always tell us what is next, He just wants us to sense that there is a next? Do you get feelings that what you're doing is right for now, but not right for long? Isn't it the coolest thought to know God drops hints that the scope of His work includes us, but it's bigger and lasts longer than we last! We just need a few bumps in the road to re-calibrate us to reality.

If you drive, then you've hit those annoying bumps in the road that someone put there intentionally — not potholes that resulted from hard winters, heavy loads, or aging highways, but attention getters designed to recalibrate your perception of the world around you to something you can't afford to miss.

Sometimes they're grooves on the edge of the road; other times they're a series of parallel bumps across the driving lane, or a single big hump in the road you can't miss. The highway system put them there to keep you from drifting, or to wake you up to a curve you were unaware of. Maybe a construction zone lies ahead and you can't afford to buzz through it. Those features of the road do their part to get your attention. They can't keep you from doing the wrong thing, but they do warn you before you do it.

Sometimes Cinderella's dad needs a bump in the road to recalibrate to reality. An "Oh please, Daddy please!" from our little girls is all we need. When I hear the opening lyrics of Steven Curtis Chapman's "Cinderella" that describe a busy dad hearing that plea, it serves as a bump in my road and puts a lump in my throat every time.

Sometimes a church's pastor needs a bump in the road as well. Our own little world desensitizes us to the bigger picture. That's exactly what God uses Isaiah to tell us: " 'For my thoughts are not your thoughts, neither are your ways my ways,' declares the LORD" (Isaiah 55:8). I don't believe Isaiah is suggesting we can never think like God thinks or that we can't follow the path God wants us to take. I do believe he's explaining that it doesn't come natural. So expect some bumps in the road to recalibrate your reality.

THE MASTER ENGINEER OF BUMPS IN THE ROAD

Nobody does bumps in the road like God. As jolting as they can be in real time, they always make sense when we wake up or get down the road.

Let me ask you this question: When was the last time you hit a God-placed speed bump that served as a reality check to your purpose as a pastor and pointed at the dwindling time you had left to work on it? When did you first come to realize you weren't going to have enough time to finish what the eternal God started?

I hit two different speed bumps separated by a few hundred yards and a full five years. God put them both there and each served a separate purpose. I hit one at the beginning of the day, the second at the end of the day. The first was to recalibrate my approach to His plans. The second was to recalibrate my schedule to His timing.

I want to share both experiences with you because I believe God will find the best way to do exactly the same thing for you. Since we aren't natural at it, God has to intervene to get us on the same page and pace with Him.

HITTING BUMPS WHEN YOU LEAST EXPECT THEM

Both speed bumps I hit were a shock to the system, fully unexpected in the moment. Each speed bump jarred me to attention as I rolled up to yet another red light, though from different directions, yet at the same crossroads — an intersection that would become an unsuspected sweet spot for me.

The place to which I am referring has since become the current site of our church campus. Crossroads is located on a corner of one of the busiest intersections in north central Indiana. It certainly lies at the doorway of Kokomo. The location has been strategic to our success and prophetic to our mission. A survey committee charged with securing the best property to relocate our growing ministry did not choose that site — God did. The property had a hill God secured for His own purposes from its creation. He had simply been waiting for the right people to catch up with His plan.

HITTING BUMPS THAT RECALIBRATE YOUR GPS

When was the last time you got a message from heaven that God was recalculating your route? God's purposes never change, but the routes He takes to get us there certainly do. Was it a relocation of the campus site? Was it a revamp of the missional strategy? Was it a revision to weekend worship, methods to connect people to each other, or approaches to invite individuals to serve in the vision? You already have the experience that preps you for the fact that those kinds of bumps aren't one and done attention getters. Though some are bigger than others, the type of bumps in question serve to recalibrate our GPS.

My first speed bump was a big one. It sent a message from heaven bearing the GPS coordinates of our new home: a corner of the intersection I was approaching and the crossroads of S.R. 26 and U.S. 31. It began with my instant frustration of hitting that aggravating red stoplight for the umpteenth time. It seemed like it could see me coming and loved to see the color of my face match the color of my brake lights.

That bump in the road turned out to be the Great Shepherd calling my attention to the traffic, as well as the roads they were travelling. Jesus said His sheep recognize His voice (John 10:27). The voice I heard in that moment was His and I instantly recognized it. I heard Him speak loud enough to drown out the conversation I was having with the stoplight. He distinctly said, "There are people on roads they don't want to travel, headed for places they don't want to go. You pull up beside them every time you stop and you pay no attention to who they are or give a thought to what they're going through. I want you to give them an option right here at this *crossroads*."

Busted. I had been seeing cars, rather than people. I had been nego- tiating them as traffic impeding my progress on busy days. God wanted me to change my view and see them as people who were sick of where they were, nervous about where they were headed, and looking for a meaningful exit to a better direction and a more meaningful destination. They wanted something better, and God was calling Crossroads to give them an exit and an access in the same moment of their willingness to change.

God gave substance to that vision with an immediate awareness of the property directly to my right, consisting of 115 acres on the southeast corner of U.S. 31 and State Road 26. It had never crossed my mind before that day. I had travelled that road all of my life and never paid attention to what looked like no more than a cornfield to the shortsighted eye. I'm not sure I ever would have really noticed it, except for that bump in the road. In a few short seconds, I knew God tasked us to make that corner our new home. I already knew our mission: to meet people where they were and help them to take their next step with Christ. This move was a practical step in relocating our campus to get closer to where they were and then better position us to help them after we got there.

HITTING BUMPS THAT RECALIBRATE YOUR TIMEPIECES

Remember the story of the man who ran into the train station panting as he looked at his watch? "What time does the seven o'clock train leave?" he said to the ticket master.

"It *left* at seven o'clock."

That's not how you want to look back on your transition. Expect to hit as many bumps in the road as necessary until you realize you need to recalibrate your watch to God's timing. The fact that you're searching for ways to complete a healthy transition tells me you've been jolted into a sense of timing by something. What you've maybe interpreted as a proverbial traffic hazard or travel imposition might have a deeper message.

Five years after I hit the first bump in the road, I hit another. And it was at the same stoplight. God's voice was unmistakable, and I heard it again. We'd purchased the property I previously described, officials had approved the plans for the new building, and the site was already being prepared. I was about to discover that the plans our church was following had already been set in motion long before I became aware of them.

When I pulled up to the stoplight, I was in the middle of listening to a sermon on the radio by Dr. David Jeremiah.

"Every great vision has deep roots," he said.

God began to speak to me. "Do you know where you are?" Of course I did. I was on the beaten path of my everyday life. I was in the community in which I had grown up. I was on the road the girl I married lived on when we dated. It was the same road on which the church I had pastored for over twenty-five years was located.

But I should have known God wasn't being trite or suggesting He might need my help to orient Himself. A certainty swept over me. *I'm at the exact same crossroads where God had led another man to start Cross-roads over 150 years ago.* I had given no thought about how God was returning our church one mile back down the same road to their first location all those years ago.

"I've been thinking about this a lot longer than you have," God said. "You didn't start it and you won't finish it. But you have a role to play in the process of it."

God had not waited 140 years for me to start the church I had been pastoring. He reminded me that I wasn't the first person He had used in His "Kokomo, Indiana Plan." He had connected me to a vision He first shared with a man of God a century and a half before He had said anything about it to me. And He affirmed every faithful man and woman who had carried that vision from Uriah McQueen, our church's founder, to Jeff Harlow.

With that bump, I knew that the plans we had for Crossroads were in alignment with the plans God had set in motion generations earlier to express His love for our community. We were spending more money than we had. We were building facilities that stretched our imagination. We were planning for more people than we had the capacity to shepherd. But we were right back where He had started us, doing exactly what He had called Uriah to do. Our mission was still precisely the same as the one that birthed us.

Oddly enough, I also knew I wouldn't always be there. God was setting eternity in my heart and recalibrating my watch to verify that some-day I would be a part of the Crossroads history as well.

"You won't finish it."

That night God set the alarm on my watch that would signal the end of my role in His plans for Crossroads. Honestly, my instantaneous re-sponse was, *Really? You can get along without me?* You are probably thinking what God was thinking right about then, and I'll give you the ben-efit of the doubt and call that look on your face a smile.

When I stop to think about it, God has always had a Joshua for a Moses and a Timothy for a Paul. So it shouldn't have been a newsflash that God could get along without me. It's not that He's utilitarian in our partner-ships with Him. His ways and thoughts are higher than ours. I suspect that God's plans sometimes take longer than the lifespan of one leader to demonstrate it was really Him, and not some human, doing it all along.

Whatever anyone thought about the success of Crossroads and the role Jeff Harlow had played in it, my transition out of it would once again serve notice to our community that this church was really the work of God, and an extension of His love to them.

God's way is to ask us to do things that are bigger than we can do alone and can't do without Him. His way is to invite us into projects that take longer than we have. Because of that, we might need to hit intermittent bumps in the road — bumps that send a message that the road is curving and we need to adjust our direction; bumps to prepare us for the fact that there really is someone waiting in the wings to continue our work after we're gone. It's not a matter of if, but when.

Thank God for engaging you in something that's too important to fade after you do.

You believe that, don't you? The basis of a healthy transition is the notion that what we're doing is worth doing and worth continuing by someone else after we're gone.

Logic kept me aware that my day to step away as the senior pastor was a scheduled event on God's calendar. I just didn't know when until what I call "the first email" slipped into my inbox. It was an inquiry I would have most likely overlooked had God not gone to remarkable measures to recalibrate my watch with a bump in the road.

Don't be afraid of those bumps in the road. Don't get frustrated when you hit them. Be grateful. The daddy-daughter dance God is calling you to may well serve you as it served me — a transition that adds meaning and gives confirmation to the value of what you've been doing, a step that brings a beautiful closure to a precious chapter in your life, and a step that leads to yet another beautiful chapter the eternal God has planned in His eternal purpose for your eternal soul.

TIME TO REFLECT

. . . .

1) When was the last bump in the road you hit that you now think could have been an attention getter from heaven? What did it recalibrate for you?

2) How long do you envision God using your church to advance His purposes in your community?

3) Who do you trust to help you work through the concept that God can get along without you while continuing the mission of your church?

4) What steps can you take now to build confidence within your church that they can get along without you?

5) Do you get a sense that your time of transition is close, or some time off? If it's close, how long do think you might have?

CHAPTER 3

. . . .

GETTING OVER
YOUR EMOTIONS

All children, except one, grow up. They soon know that they will grow up, and the way Wendy knew was this. One day when she was two years old she was playing in a garden, and she plucked another flower and ran with it to her mother. I suppose she must have looked rather delightful, for Mrs. Darling put her hand to her heart and cried, "Oh, why can't you remain like this forever!" This was all that passed between them on the subject, but henceforth Wendy knew that she must grow up.

You always know after you are two.

Two is the beginning of the end.

– J. M. BARRIE (PETER PAN)

Peter Pan was cute, but he fought a losing battle. You can resist growing up, but you can't keep the world around you from changing. Living a full life and helping your world experience its highest potential hinges on the healthiness of the transition that bridges *what is* to *what can be*.

In all of my transitions of life, nothing compared to the heart quiver I felt on three different days catalyzed by the same question. A pastor asked that question for my daughters' weddings: "Who's come this way to give this woman to become the wife of this man?"

Three times I have stood between my little girl and the new man of her life. I was breathing the last breaths of a precious season of my life. I lived that moment over and again in my head for years before each one actually happened. I had not answered a question with such premeditation since I answered, "I do" to the pastor asking me a question while at the side of my bride: "Do you take this woman to be your wife?"

Now the question was similar, but so different. He was asking me to *give*, not *take*, and the woman was my daughter, not my future wife: "Who comes this way to *give* this woman (my little girl) to become the wife of this man? I knew the appropriate answer was, "Her mother and I do," but I wasn't thinking much about her mother right about then. This was between me, the preacher, and Prince Charming!

I needed no cue card for the words that were mine to speak. I knew them by heart. Any Peter Pan kind of hesitation in answering the question would have only brought confusion. I knew my daughters were growing up before I heard that question, but there was no escaping it once the preacher asked it. One at a time, all three of my little Wendys had celebrated that second birthday. It was their wedding day, and I knew we had long since passed "the beginning of the end." I knew it would never be the same again.

Frankly, God's plan for marriage demands it's never the same again. Jesus reaffirmed the original plan outlined in Genesis when He told man to leave his father and mother and become one with his wife (Genesis 2:24). After teaching kids to honor their dad and mom, the New Testament teaches that wives are to become aligned with their husbands (Ephesians 5:22). Transition doesn't get bigger than that.

Little did I know that the new would fulfill the old and open Becky and me up to a new season of possibilities. Gone were car insurance and tuition bills. With the arrival of grandkids, back were little league games and loud holidays. But in that transitional moment from what had been to what would be, as beautiful as the wedding scene was, it was one of the hardest things I ever did. My Cinderella was about to become Prince Charming's princess.

So let me ask again, why do we struggle with transition?

YOUR EMOTIONS ARE THE GREATEST THREAT TO TRANSITION

In all of the complexities of transition, nothing gets closer to the core of the challenge than dealing with the emotions it stirs. Your personal emotions will arguably be your most threatening nemesis and, without question, a tricky step in the daddy-daughter dance of your transition. You can break transition down to a series of strategic steps to be taken methodically that, on paper, will get you to the end of a process. But it's that human part of you that can rear up and put you out of sync with your partner's best interests.

James minces no words in reminding us that our human nature can arise in the best of us and at the most spiritual of times. He points toward one of the heroes of the faith and says, "Elijah was a man just like us. He prayed earnestly that it would not rain, and it did not rain on the land for three and a half years" (James 5:17).

James uses a compound word, *homoiopathes*, translated by the NIV with the phrase "just like us" and it means "similarly affected." He combines the Greek word *homoios*, meaning similar (in appearance or character), with the Greek word path'-o, to experience a sensation or impression (usually painful).

You don't need anyone to tell you that pastors are fully human and we experience the same kinds of painful sensations and impressions that all people do. Emotions are part of the equation when working out the formula for a healthy transition. Every dad at his daughter's wedding and every leader going through transition must keep his eyes wide open when it comes to being transparent about his emotions.

Transparency is vital in transition. Your first step in this dance is to anticipate and identify the emotions you will feel. Then you must take whatever time and effort you need to work through them. You don't need to try to do this by yourself. Keep a God-friend close, and then determine to lead through the emotions. Cinderella will be fighting emotions of her own. They will need you to lead with a clear head and a confident step.

You know your normal emotional responses, but don't be surprised if they don't follow the path of grief. You may be taking a step up the ladder and the emotions are all happy ones, but if you're either moving off a rung that you've enjoyed, or stepping off the ladder altogether, you're sustaining a loss. You're going to grieve it at some level. I can alert you to the possibilities by sharing with you the emotions I felt along the way.

DISAPPOINTMENT AND SADNESS

I couldn't deny it. Neither emotion was dominant, but disappointment and the future with commensurate sadness tinted the glasses through which I viewed the past. There were barriers we hadn't broken and plateaus we hadn't escaped. A leader looks beyond those impediments with an eye that believes they are temporary. I felt a new empathy for Moses as he climbed Mt. Nebo: certain His people were going to get there, aware he would not share the success with them.

I started as a 20-year-old. By my 55th birthday, I noticed a difference. My voice seemed too familiar to my peers and uninspiring to the younger generation. I began to hear about people who weren't connecting because of me. Younger leaders seemed unimpressed with my approach and priorities. They were never disrespectful, but every sign indicated they were no longer interested in what I was thinking.

Cinderella was growing up and she needed to go places I wasn't able to take her. She needed a prince, not a dad.

ENVY

Envy had not historically been a battle for me, but in this unfamiliar turf, I heard its snarl from the shadow side of my soul at the oddest times. I occasionally walked out of meetings leaving some wondering where I stood, but I never walked into a meeting with the team wondering where I sat. The first time the new prince sat down in my king's chair, I heard myself snarl. I joined the rookie razzing, but I hoped no one heard the snarl in my soul. How would I explain having the gracious thought, *Hey, I'm not dead yet! Who in the world do you think you are, sitting in my chair?*

The loudest envy snarl I heard came when it dawned on me that Chris was going to hear God's heart for the next steps of Crossroads before I did. I could take you to the various sweet spots on this planet where God had given me clear direction about the future of the church I was leading. God doesn't like using middlemen to relay key messages from heaven to His leaders. It is never a good thing when you read about Him doing it in the Bible. That preference wasn't going to change with me after Chris put on the leadership mantle.

Envy can make you feel like a two-year-old brat. It was yours, now it's his, and you want it back. Or maybe he has something you wanted and never got; now he's getting it and you want it. Either way, you feel cheated; left out.

When your goal is a healthy transition, envy will always create problems. James warns that untamed envy will play havoc with the outcome. He writes, "For where you have envy and selfish ambition, there you find disorder and every evil practice" (James 3:16). Don't ignore the snarl. That dog has teeth.

FEAR

Every transition has its woods, and every forest has the fear monster lurking in the shadows. I heard a snapping twig and felt a twitch while taking more than one step on this path. Bigfoot may only be in your head, but the thought of him does something to your feet. The fight or flight syndrome is real. Fear can stop you when you need to take your next step and it can cause you to bolt when you need to pause. It's no good when it becomes your dance partner.

I feared history being lost, alteration of core values, and a shifted focus. I feared people not staying connected and slipping through the transitional cracks. We'll talk more about it later, but I had my moments when I wondered if Chris was everything I had thought. There's nothing like fear to give you unhealthy second thoughts.

The year before I introduced Chris to the church was the hardest year of my life. I feared that the struggle had simply taken its toll, won the day, and was running me out of town. I even overheard whispers of that coming from others. I feared feeling unfulfilled and discontented after the transition was over.

I feared becoming irrelevant to Chris, Crossroads, and God's plan, both as a lame duck before I left and an old computer after I was gone.

I had to listen to another voice, or this Beelzebub would turn my journey into a living nightmare. Thank God for what He said through John to address our fears when he wrote, "There is no fear in love. But perfect love drives out fear, because fear has to do with punishment. The one who fears is not made perfect in love" (1 John 4:18).

I love Max Lucado's quote on dealing with the kinds of anxiety fear can cause. He writes in his book *Fearless*: "Become a worry-slapper. Treat frets like mosquitoes. Do you procrastinate when a bloodsucking bug lights on your skin? 'I'll take care of it in a moment.' Of course you don't! You give the critter the slap it deserves. Be equally decisive with anxiety."

PRIDE

After a recent snowstorm and a very long day of plowing through the huge snowdrifts it had created, I finally settled in my truck and headed for home. I had one last phone call to make before I got there, so I reached down to dial the number. Three digits before I punched the last of the numbers I felt the uneasy nudge to get my eyes back on the road. It was too late. I was at a full 45 degrees to the road and had already crossed the point of no return. I was in the ditch, with the operative word being *in*. It was late, dark, ten degrees below zero, and I was somewhere between where I started and where I was going, but not entirely sure where. I was stuck beyond all self-help. And I was not happy.

That's exactly what pride does. Pride takes your eyes off the road. The proud person's focus is on self, and that's the polar opposite of what healthy transition is all about. You don't have a clue where you're going to end up, but it's some place you're bound not to like. Eugene Peterson's paraphrase describes it this way, "First pride, then the crash — the bigger the ego, the harder the fall" (Proverbs 16:18, THE MESSAGE).

At some point, it dawned on me that a leader's vision had to be bigger than his ego. It may be tough for the person with the ego to see it, but his pride, as well as his pending catastrophe, is obvious to everyone around him. Pride leads to chaos, not beautiful choreography.

Ego turned Lucifer into a monster. That monster lurked in Eden and turned the whole world into a kind of maelstrom.

Jack Hayford teaches that fear and pride are close traveling companions. I never found that to be more obvious than I did on some of the darker nights of this transition. Not only did I have to confront fears about my future, but I also came to realize that I was hypersensitive to other people's expectation of my success. Over time I had drifted into trying to live up to what they thought was the promise of my life.

I read once of a person who said he had discovered a dimension of pride he hadn't thought about before. He described it as a preoccupation with what people thought about him. This form of pride dominates with an intimidating fear that a person will never meet anyone's expectations.

Pride comes in a thousand different odors, but it stinks in every case. Use your nose and God will help you sniff it out. Don't take another step on this all important path until you pour out your uneasy soul before the Lord, and beg Him with the passion of a once burned David as he bowed before God and cried from the depths of his soul, "Search me, O God, and know my heart; test me and know my anxious thoughts. See if there is any offensive way in me, and lead me in the way everlasting"

(Psalm 139:23-24).

God was as instrumental in forming your Cinderella as He was in creating the rest of the world. You've done nothing to warrant pride. Don't allow the monster to crash the celebration of God's work through you and in your church, and spoil the blessing of enjoying it for another generation.

If this is the dance God's called you to, then the emotions that a transition stirs can be taken in stride. They don't have to determine the last steps with your little girl. They don't have to spoil a beautiful time.

You need to answer the following two questions during your transition: Do you really give your baby girl to this man? How do you fully give her into the care of someone else?

Take a breath and keep reading.

TIME TO REFLECT

. . . .

1) What first comes to mind when you think about handing over the reins of leadership to a new leader, even if he is a Prince Charming?

2) What do you think might be your greatest emotional challenge to initiate transition?

3) Who is that person or small circle with whom you could share your emotions?

4) What steps do you need to take to develop that level of relationship?

5) When can you begin that process?

CHAPTER 4

. . . .

IDENTIFYING CINDERELLA

> *No one shall be my wife but she whose foot this golden slipper fits.*
>
> – (Brothers Grimm, *Cinderella*,
> Translated by Margaret Taylor)

By this time, you are aware that the future of the vision and organization you've been leading should outlast your tenure. It is clear that a leadership transition has moved up your to-do list. You've started working through the emotions that assignment generates. Your next step in a healthy transition is identifying Cinderella.

This may seem like such a "duh" point, yet failure to define and identify Cinderella may well rank as the number one terrorist to transition plans.

The enigma of this step is that it only requires an acknowledgement of the obvious. We are leaders. Making the shortlist of aptitudes for leadership is the ability to identify and keep the team focused on the main thing. If you don't have a knack for getting that right, God or the church might remove, not replace, you.

If you're acquainted with the original story of Cinderella and Prince

Charming, the original fair maiden had her own identity theft problems. Her stepsisters caused some confusion and volunteered for the Cinderella position after her chaotic exit from the ball. Thank goodness for the unsuspecting wit of her fairy godmother. Like any fashionista, her wardrobe designer had dressed her to the hilt, completing her outfit with original slippers. That fashion detail set her apart and set her up for the love of her life. In Cinderella's case, the old adage "If the shoe fits, wear it" allowed for a happy ending. The slipper fits only the one for whom it was designed. In the case of your transition, the slipper fits but one foot.

The parallel of the prince exhausting the guest list in an attempt to find the one who had captured his heart is an interesting one. We must develop our own course of action to find the one whose foot fits in the slipper and then settle for nobody less. Miss it and you mess with the end of the story. Miss it and, at the least, you will change the trajectory of your church.

A CINDERELLA OF THE BUSINESS WORLD

The business world can confuse leadership transition just as much as the church world. The results can be painful, if not catastrophic.

One of the biggest business debacles in corporate history played out, in no small part, in the small city in which Crossroads is located. My brother was a firsthand witness. Brian has spent his entire career working for Chrysler Corporation under its many ownerships and CEOs. He started as a gauge reader and will end his career as Vice President - Head of NAFTA Manufacturing, FCA - North America. Believe me; he's been through the highs and lows of the company.

Brian and I have talked extensively of the series of events that began in 1992 and ended in bankruptcy in 2009. There were shifts in business paradigms, economic downturns, and labor agreements that contributed to the final disaster, but my brother lays the bulk of the blame on leadership that failed to keep the company aligned with its core values and on course with its missional purpose.

Lee Iacocca recognized a Cinderella when he saw her, and turned Chrysler around from near insolvency into a strong car manufacturing company. He believed Cinderella was Chrysler's team of leadership and laborers who were sacrificially committed to the vision of manufacturing cars people wanted to buy, were proud to own, and safe to drive. Brian described those early years under Iacocca's leadership as a time when the company not only built cars driven by those core values, but also built personal pride in the employees by being part of a quality company. They needed governmental assistance to pull off a turnaround from the hard times of the '70s, but Chrysler's chief led them out of impending demise into an industrial dream team.

Shortly after announcing the end of his tenure, Iacocca would characterize his successor as a leader who knew how to refine existing processes with a focus on profits. Brian described Iacocca's successor as a mild-mannered, consensus builder, but better at making money than building cars. The difference is so subtle, but the focus was a critical shift. Building great cars makes money and creates jobs. When making money is the primary objective and the bottom line becomes the focus, cutting corners and compromising standards can jeopardize building great cars. The new manufacturing chief was so successful in those first years that Forbes named Chrysler "Company of the Year" and *Industry Week* named Chrysler among the 100 best-managed companies.

But after Chrysler was sold to Daimler in a 1998 "merger of equals" that ended disastrously, Iacocca later said that hand-picking the man he chose as his replacement was the biggest mistake of his life.

It wasn't until after Iacocca's initial successor left in 2000 that it became evident that he had taken his eye off the product and the morale of his people, and merged with another auto company driven by disparate agendas and a dissimilar culture. As part of the deal with Daimler, Chrysler's name was diminished, its cash reserves were plundered, and the merger produced little or no shared product or cross branding. The debate of his wisdom and intent will rage on, but regardless, his influence forever changed the course of Chrysler. My brother believes he never got a handle on who Cinderella really was.

The last CEO of Chrysler as a publicly held company finally jettisoned the automaker into the hands of Cerberus, who cared nothing for the company's legacy, leaders, laborers, or future. Cerberus only cared about what it could strip for profits through a leveraged buyout.

Brian describes his present position as the privilege of his professional career: working under the leadership of Sergio Marchionne. Without hesitation, he classifies Sergio as the greatest business mind and industrial leader on the planet. It took his leadership, a bailout from our government, a great leadership team, the commitment of the labor force, and God's blessing for Chrysler to come back as it has. And at the heart of it was a return to its original purpose and core values: to design, build, and sell great products that customers want to drive and are proud to own; and to restore the value of the leadership team and labor force that produces them.

This example may serve the next chapter equally well when we look at finding Prince Charming, but it certainly confirms the dangers of failing to rightly identify Cinderella. Tens of thousands of workers would have lost their jobs and many more their benefits, the American auto industry would have lost a corporate icon, and millions of happy vehicle owners would be driving a different truck or car today had Marchionne and company not rediscovered the genuine Cinderella of their story.

Building great cars with good people was Iacocca's Cinderella. Sergio Marchionne has found the foot that fits the slipper once again.

As important as successful companies, careers, and job opportunities are, nothing is more devastating than the toll taken on the eternal when church leaders get confused about Cinderella's identity. God has too much riding on the role His churches play in His plans to sit idly by and watch us mess it up without intervention. That explains why He was so clear about my future transition.

Go back with me to that night God brightened the lights and directed my attention to the time gap between the end of my tenure and the fulfillment of His plans through Crossroads. The words were clear and specific: "I've been thinking about this a lot longer than you have. You didn't start it, and you won't finish it. You have a role to play in the process of it."

To manage the tensions the transition would likely create I needed some help getting beyond the you. Most of us have a preoccupation with self, but this is one of those circumstances in which a failure in that area of vulnerability can be devastating to the outcome. I could not get stuck on you. The night I've described is evidence of God's willingness to go to extraordinary measures to ensure I didn't.

To get beyond the *you* I had to start thinking about the *it*.

Here are two questions to ask yourself to help you do just that: Who calls your church home? What is the role God has chosen her to play in His plans? The answers will distinguish her from everyone and everything else. Those answers will mark the *it* that Jesus loved and gave His life for. Those answers will specify what Jesus is building and what hell cannot stop.

DETERMINE WHO CINDERELLA *ISN'T*

IT *ISN'T* YOU

God never made me wonder if He still loved me, or if He had a future for me, but He cleared up any confusion I might have had: *It* wasn't me.

It reminds me of my daughters' wedding days. Though it sure feels like it (after all, you are the dad, the prince asked you for permission, and you are potentially paying for it all), the wedding is not about you. And in this case, though he's the new man in your daughter's life, and he's far from unimportant, it's not about him either. The wedding, and your part in it as a dad, is about your daughter and her future. After all, from the time you heard a doctor would place her in your arms in just a few months, though she's brought you immeasurable joy throughout her childhood and adolescence, it's always been about her.

If the transition is all about you, then it becomes nothing more than securing your personal future. If all you want is out and being able to land with your feet on the ground, then there are plenty of ways to do the "get-out-of-here" thing. Just don't confuse any of those objectives with making a healthy transition of a church into a season of new leadership the priority.

IT *ISN'T* YOUR SUCCESSOR

Finding Prince Charming deserves every moment it takes. The future senior leader deserves plenty of attention after you discover him. His personal transition from where he is, and all that it takes to set him up to win, deserves every resource at your disposal. But make no mistake — this transition is about the future of your church.

It's a black flag, not just a red one, if you see indications that the person you're considering sees himself as the focus of this transition. Don't open a gate to which you hold the keys and escort a self-seeking imposter of a shepherd to fleece the sheep, rather than seeing to their best interests.

IT *ISN'T* YOUR DENOMINATIONAL LEADERSHIP

Though they could very well be significant stakeholders in the decision, denominational leadership isn't the focus *of* the transition. They can serve as meaningful resources with vested interests, but unhealthy things happen when they forget they are role-players and you allow them to overstep their boundaries.

GET CLEAR ABOUT WHO CINDERELLA *IS*

IT IS YOUR CHURCH

I've sat in hundreds of homes and had hundreds of more people sit in mine. Every conversation with people expressing interest in Crossroads as their future church home ended by quoting a paraphrase of Paul, "But now hath God set the members every one of them in the body, as it hath pleased him" (1 Corinthians 12:18, KJV). I not only believe that God picks the place, but also that he joins them to the other people. Paul also said, "In whom all the building fitly framed together groweth unto a holy temple in the Lord" (Ephesians 2:21, KJV).

"Fitly framed" describes a tongue and groove kind of process joining people into a tight relationship with the others in the same body. I wanted them to understand that they weren't alone, and that their connections with others were intentional and strategic.

Since I believe God had everything to do with who Crossroads is, then it was easy to mark who it was when it came to identifying our Cinderella. If the evidence demonstrated in any way that Crossroads was, or might be, their home, then they were *it*.

You may track people with the use of an official membership roll. You may develop your list of people from a composite of official, potential, and closet members. However you count them, they are *it*.

IT HAS PERSONAL NAMES

Cinderella is the metaphor of choice for this book. *It* is the pronoun God used to focus my attention on Crossroads when the time came for the pending leadership transition. But make no mistake, real people with real names make up the "who." Each one is a part of Cinderella with their own name and a personal story.

So when the Holy Spirit made sure I understood that it wasn't me, I had no trouble concluding who it was. It had names — thousands of them: George and Angie, Mike and Wendy, Phil the police officer and Barb the evangelist, Dennis the coach and Jody the card writer, Becky the calligrapher, Chad the new believer, Tony the smiler, Amber the Snicker's girl, Lisa the writer, and on and on.

It has personal names, and it would serve both you and the process well if you started writing them down: names from every age bracket; names from every point on the spiritual maturity continuum; names from every ring of church growth; names from every type of human struggle;

names from every category of spiritual gifts. Make your list.

If you take the time to ask the Holy Spirit who *it* is, I promise you that He already knows who they are and will start calling them by name when you ask. It may seem contradictory to make such a deal about the "who," only to follow it with a "what," but as stated earlier, I believe Cinderella is both a "who" and a "what." You must be equally clear concerning what *it is* and what *it isn't*.

STIPULATE WHAT CINDERELLA *ISN'T*

IT ISN'T PROGRAMMING

Programming is important. It is where the rubber meets the road in your mission. It is a must to align programming with your core values. It demands strategizing to maximize effectiveness. It will get well-deserved attention in a later chapter. But for all it is, programming is not *it*.

IT ISN'T TRADITION

Tradition is not to be confused with heritage. Tradition is a "how," whereas heritage is a "what." Tradition can be included in heritage and given a place of respect, but you can't view it as a permanent formula for a desired outcome.

Sometimes God intentionally changes an approach to the execution of a strategy in alignment with a core value. He doesn't want us to get caught up in the *how* and miss the *what* because we don't understand the *why*.

Jesus upset the applecart when He pushed back against the Pharisees and their tradition. What He said caught Matthew's attention and the Holy Spirit jogged his memory when he wrote his gospel. Matthew records that Jesus shocked the spiritual leaders of that day by saying, "...you nullify the word of God for the sake of your tradition" (Matthew 15:6).

"Because it's the way we've always done it" is the bane of every new leader, but the same web can entangle us. You *know* it's the worst of reasons to do even the right thing.

God taught Moses that painful lesson (Numbers 20:6-11). Compare it to the record of the earlier event recorded in Exodus 17:6. You can bet that if God changed the delivery system on Moses when fetching water for the Israelites in a crisis, then He will switch it up on us. He never wants us to get confused as to why we are so blessed. Tradition can get in the way.

Many traditions will survive in a healthy leadership transition, but make no mistake about it: Tradition is not *it*.

SPECIFY WHAT CINDERELLA *IS*

IT IS YOUR CORE VALUES

Core values are those elements that Jesus called treasures; things so valuable to us that we put them in special places for easy access and safe-keeping. He cut to the chase by saying, "For where your treasure is, there your heart will be also" (Matthew 6:21).

Cut your Cinderella and she will bleed her core values. As "...the life of the body is in its blood" (Leviticus 17:11, NLT), so the life of all we do as a church is in our core values.

Core values are the building blocks for achieving predictability and consistency in the actions that bring about the results we want. A vision is no more than a daydream if you do not base it on your church's core values. The mission statement is no more than a platitude if you don't birth it out of your core values.

What is core to your church? Cut your leadership team and the people who make it happen and what do they bleed? Those life-giving values must be noted and treated with respect as part of the *what* in your leadership transition. Tinker with the core values and you change who the church is. If you fail to nurture and celebrate those values, your church will suffer from a type of spiritual anemia. Your core values must transcend every leadership transition. They are what *it* is.

IT IS YOUR MISSION

Not only does the Bible teach that God has a unique place for each person in your church, but His plan also determines the unique place your church fills in the world as He extends His goodness and grace to it.

John shares a vision that gives a description of the relationship between Jesus and His church. He says, "I turned around to see the voice that was speaking to me. And when I turned I saw seven golden lampstands, and among the lampstands was someone like a son of man" (Revelation 1:12-13).

That scene gives added insights to the stern warning to the church at Ephesus: "If you do not repent, I will come to you and remove your lampstand from its place" (Revelation 2:5).

No book gives more insight as to the position, structure, and role of the church than the book of Ephesians. The church of Ephesus had outstanding leaders in its early days. The Bible notes its people's giftedness. God positioned it as light in one of the darkest places in the world. It had a powerful impact during that stage in its life. *The church made the list in the Book of Revelation, for crying out loud!* No lampstand had cast more light than the church at Ephesus.

How astounding to hear this grave warning. How shocking to know the church ignored the warning, and neglected what had been core to the point that Jesus seemingly did remove it from that central place in His plan to give light to a dark world. How staggering to know there is not a sign of a believer, let alone a church, where that once great beacon stood. They didn't just relocate; God removed them from their position.

Shouldn't we be asking the question, "When did the church of Ephesus drop the ball?" Could it have been during one of its leadership transitions? Could it be that the leadership fixed its attention on something else, and that's why the congregation is told, "Yet I hold this against you: You have forsaken your first love" (Revelation 2:4)?

I can't live with the thought of the lights of Crossroads going out. Talk about rolling over in your grave! I can't tolerate the possibility that Crossroads could lose its place of significance in God's plan at any point until Jesus comes. I don't even want to think about that hill and our facilities that have stood as a place of hope becoming anything less than what it is today, let alone having all of its signs removed to the point that it never even existed.

Our mission statement describes our place in the lampstand: *"Meeting people where they are and helping them take their next step with Christ."* It is foundational to the explanation of everything we do. It provides the catalyst for asking questions in consideration of what we are not doing, but need to. It provides the fortitude to say no to the things that are nice, but not necessary. That mission is at the heart of Crossroads. It kept the church on course during earlier seasons of transition, it kept it on course during my tenure, and it will keep it on course long after they've forgotten about me.

You have to think about your place in the lampstand. What is Jesus' purpose for your church? What is your church doing that would break His heart and leave your community poorer if the leaders drop that purpose during the leadership transition?

Our mission is at the heart of what *it* is.

IT IS YOUR VISION

Your values drive you, and your mission directs you. Your vision inspires you to persist in what you believe and do, and it has to transcend the leadership transition. Your vision must be clear and intact; you must be able to articulate it to your successor, because vision is a huge part of what *it* is.

IT IS YOUR COLLECTIVE GIFTS AND INDIVIDUAL CALLINGS

After Jesus defeated our enemy on his own turf, our King ascended into heaven and gave gifts to people, enabling each person to participate in a meaningful way what He does through His church. The work of the Spirit distributes those gifts among us (Ephesians 4:8).

Let these verses sink into your soul:

"A spiritual gift is given to each of us so we can help each other" (1 Corinthians 12:7, NLT).

"However, he has given each one of us a special gift through the generosity of Christ . . . Now these are the gifts Christ gave to the church . . . As each part does its own special work, it helps the other parts grow, so that the whole body is healthy and growing and full of love" (Ephesians 4:7, 11, 16, NLT).

"Just as our bodies have many parts and each part has a special function, so it is with Christ's body. We are many parts of one body, and we all belong to each other. In his grace, God has given us different gifts for doing certain things well" (Romans 12:4-6, NLT).

Those gifts don't belong to any one person; they belong to the entire body. Those gifts are so precious and powerful that they must be deeply regarded. They weren't meant for a season, but for a purpose. As certainly as those gifts transcend seasons, they are meant to transcend leadership transitions.

The aggregate gifts residing in the people God placed in your church to accomplish the purpose He assigned is woven into the fabric of what *it* is.

IT IS YOUR HERITAGE

Please don't confuse tradition with heritage. We've already determined they are not the same. But just as every person has a story, so does every church. And just as understanding a person requires you to know his or her story, so understanding a church demands you know its story.

God never intended for our heritage to become a roof, but rather a foundation. We don't have to be afraid of esteeming our church's heritage if we don't get confused as to its place in shaping our future. The heritage of Crossroads is extremely rich: as of this writing, it contains 167 years of stories of ordinary people doing extraordinary things. Keeping your heritage in the picture helps you connect the dots and to see you aren't an upstart with God, but that He's been thinking about this a lot longer than you have.

Take the time to storyboard your church heritage. Few things are more encouraging. It's like pulling out the yellowing family albums with their tattered pictures and showing them to the next generation.

Your story must transcend your leadership transition, because your heritage gives character to what it is. Don't take another step until you've settled in your soul *who* and *what* Cinderella is. I would encourage you to read no further until you write your own description of the precious people and timeless purpose of your church. Your answer is at the heart of this transition.

IF YOU'RE NOT THE ONE LEAVING

If you're on the leadership team and your outgoing leader is missing it, for heaven's sake sit him down and talk about your concerns. The Bible says it best, "As iron sharpens iron, so one man sharpens another" (Proverbs 27:17). The sparks may need to fly now, because if not now, then I guarantee they will later.

As an important side note, there is something that separates you as the transition team apart from the transitioning leader. God or the church may task you with playing the role of taking care of that outgoing leader. When it's obvious that somebody else is fully engaged in taking care of the outgoing leader, it greatly reduces his temptation to take care of himself. He can't make the Cinderella dance about himself, but you can make it a special moment for him. During the transition, that leader deserves for the church to honor him for his role in the life of the people and purpose of the church. Even wedding days have their celebrated father-daughter dance when no one else shares the floor. You're the ones to make sure your outgoing leader's transition to a new reality without you is as happy as your new reality without him. This may well be harder on your outgoing leader than you know. Reward him for his selfless approach to his departure.

REMEMBER WHOSE DANCE IT IS

Once identified, keep a picture of Cinderella on the wall. When I pray for my kids and grandkids each morning, I picture them as I speak their names. Photos are plastered all over my office walls and sitting on my shelves. Pictures are powerful.

Do whatever it takes to keep the who and what front line and center in this process. It can get frustrating, but as leaders, we are susceptible to such immersion in the process that we forget whose dance it is.

Bill Hybels prompts us to keep vision fresh for people. In his book *Axiom: Powerful Leadership Proverbs*, he reminds us that "vision leaks." Our people can get an idea who Cinderella is and what the transition is all about, but then forget if you don't keep reminding them. Working to keep people and programs in alignment with the vision is mandatory to staying true to the task.

These may be bases we didn't have to cover since they are so fundamental to leadership, but please never forget this: *The little slipper fits only one foot.* Others may try it on and wear it, but bloody feet and hobbled steps will make it obvious in the end, if not at the beginning.

And though it may sting to think this leadership transition is not about you as the outgoing leader, never forget the God-honored role you've played with Cinderella. He entrusted her into your care. He believed in you to love Him by loving His cherished church. He promised never to forget all that you've done for His Cinderella when the writer of Hebrews wrote,

"God is not unjust; he will not forget your work and the love you have shown him as you have helped his people and continue to help them" (Hebrews 6:10).

No other person on the planet knows Cinderella as you do. That's why you have to make sure this process is thorough. Make her nothing more and nothing less than who and what she really is.

No, you're not Cinderella, but God let you dance with her.

TIME TO REFLECT

. . . .

1) Take the time to think through and identify the demographics of your church. Who do you believe might be most vulnerable during a time of leadership transition?

2) What Kingdom purposes does God use you to serve in your community?

3) What are your church's core values?

4) What are the areas of giftedness in your church, and who are the gift-bearers?

5) What are the highlights of your church's heritage?

CHAPTER 5

. . . .

FINDING PRINCE CHARMING

An army of a thousand is easy to find, but,
ah, how difficult to find a general.

— CHINESE PROVERB

Fiddler on the Roof is a musical set in Tsarist Russia in 1905 and based on a Jewish family consisting of a father, a mother, and five daughters. The story centers on Tevye, the father, and his efforts to preserve his family's Jewish roots and religious traditions as his daughters respond to the pull of outside influences. He must deal with the strong-willed actions of his three older daughters — each one choosing a husband that threatened the continuity of the customs of his faith.

If you've been a player in this predicament, you will quickly identify with Tevye, the father. And Tevye truly understands the weight of the decision and the tension we leaders feel in the matchmaking process.

If you're Cinderella in this transition, you'll catch yourself identifying with the three girls of the story.

The lyrics of the song *Matchmaker* uncannily capture the emotions of the process and the stakes of the match. There's a hilarious segment of the song in which Tzeitel, the eldest daughter, throws a scarf over her head, imitating Yente, the matchmaker. She torments her sisters with descriptions of the matches she has arranged for them.

One at a time, Tzeitel mortifies her siblings with depictions of men who are older than their dad and wider than they are tall, as well as being wife-beating drunkards. She mocks them with the notion that they can't be too picky — after all, life is more than just being happy. Right? Right! What should they expect, a prince? Get real!

Among the subplots of Fiddler is the concession that every matchmaker brings vulnerabilities to the table. Any prospective bride would feel uneasy with teasing sisters and village busybodies taking their Cupid shots, but even a loving dad can bring a predisposition to the search that is scary to his little girl. Finding the right match is a riddle with the highest of stakes.

I think Hodel has the line of the hour, "Well, somebody has to arrange the matches." Well, somebody does. The question is, "How do they do it?" More poignant yet, "How do you do it?"

Fiddler addresses an issue leadership can't overlook in a healthy leadership transition. No one felt more pressure than Tevye, the strong but gentle patriarchal father of five daughters. He knew his culture and believed tradition answered every question. He also loved his daughters and wanted them to be happy. It's not healthy to ignore either one of those considerations.

YOUR CULTURE MUST DRIVE THE SEARCH

The culture of your church has to be a marker in this search. It may very well be that you're in a cultural shift, as the Jewish family in the story at hand, but you can't ignore it. It may be that no shift has occurred as of yet, but Bob Dylan is right on this one: "The Times They Are a-Changin' ". You may choose to bring in a strong leader to effect that change. If so, that has to be part of the consensus-building phase of the process. It would be a disaster to bring in a maverick for a leader to determine personally all the changes and with the executive power to implement them unilaterally.

You have undoubtedly witnessed the impact of ignored cultural differences or personality clashes on a marriage when couples have chosen to trivialize their personal natural defaults. Young couples infatuated with the surface, but impervious to their cultural diversities are headed for trouble. Natural affinities are important, but if you turn a blind eye to the deeper differences, a church is just as destined for turbulence if there's a mismatch in church leadership. It's an unwise path that ignores the warning signs from Amos' pen: "Can two people walk together without agreeing on the direction?" (Amos 3:3, NLT).

The Bible is clear. The answer is obvious, and so much easier to live with if you get the right read on each other's heading before you take the first step. The pain of a bad date or a broken engagement is nothing compared to that of a failed marriage. And we don't have to think hard to think of bad marriages between leaders and the led. It becomes a nightmare and an unhealthy situation in which no one wins.

In our Cinderella metaphor, the initial connection between the princess and the prince is her foot and his slipper. In Chapter 3, we dealt with the importance of sizing up Cinderella's foot. This chapter looks at the slipper in the prince's hand. Not every foot will fit that shoe. Some princes focus so much on finding a princess that they will gently force their slipper on Cinderella's foot and persuade her that he can make the shoe fit. Some princesses focus so much on finding a prince that they convince themselves they will get used to the slipper.

There are only two inevitable and undesirable scenarios when a mismatch is made: either the prince and his slipper have to go, or the shoe will determine the shape of Cinderella's foot. And in a society that works on the basis of the social contract, Cinderella will walk rather than dance when she finally realizes that slipper is never going to fit. If the prince doesn't leave, the princess will.

My paraphrase of Amos 3:3 is, "How can two walk together if the shoes don't fit?"

I highly recommend that you and the leadership team spend quality time with an excellent book by Carolyn Weese and J. Russell Crabtree called, *The Elephant in the Boardroom* published by Leadership Network. The authors do a particularly good job of helping you think through the culture of your church.

To be clear, a church's culture is the natural way they do things. A church's culture is observable through its behaviors; values and deeply held beliefs drive those behaviors. Over time, those behaviors become routine and develop into traditions. Church culture works like proverbial factory resets in a computer when pressures mount and things get confused and un-certain.

Working through the culture grid offered by *The Elephant in the Boardroom* is an eye-opening, yet simple, process that allows you to apply it as long as you're willing to be candid. If you're able to separate who you wish you were from who you really are, then it will be a solid step that gives you firm footing for the next one.

DETERMINING THE OTHER VARIABLE IN YOUR MARRIAGE EQUATION

Our experience at Crossroads included three phases to the discovery process of Prince Charming, all of which can be complex and lengthy. We had to describe our prince, find him, and then confirm him as a possibility with Cinderella. Yes, this boils down to a hybridized form of an arranged marriage.

DESCRIBING OUR PRINCE

I understood the culture of Crossroads, its expectations, and the demands on the leader to deliver better than anybody did. Though the choice of a prince was not mine to decide, it was mine to catalyze and to help facilitate the process of securing him. That process begins with knowing Crossroads' version of tall, dark, and handsome.

Our prince had to have a healthy home. We take seriously the instructions Paul gave to Timothy when he outlined the qualifications for a senior leader of the church: "He must manage his own family well and see that his children obey him with proper respect. (If anyone does not know how to manage his own family, how can he take care of God's church?)" (1 Timothy 3:4-5).

If he is married, his wife must be equally suited for the position. I know the unfaltering role Becky played with me, and thank God she did. The job demands of a leader's spouse do not change when the leader does. The leader's spouse is a true partner with joint ownership in this venture.

If he has children, he must demonstrate a healthy relationship with them. You don't need me to tell you that kids are born with a mind of their own, but a healthy relationship with Dad goes a long way in helping to shape their mind. His kids will not be the only humans God's charged him to shape. If the duties of fatherhood are too challenging for him, he's probably not up for the challenge of pastoring (at least at Crossroads).

Our man had to feel comfortable in our community. Our mission included more people outside of the church than inside it. He had to be flexible at minimum, if not altogether bent to fit.

Our new leader had to be experienced with leading a staff of similar size, casting vision for a ministry comparable in scope, and being able to speak effectively to a congregation of approximate scale.

Our new leader had to align with our core values before he found out what ours were. In our case, experience with kid's ministries with an emphasis on the role of parents was particularly important. His view of worship and the style he preferred for weekend services also served as an important marker for us.

Any preexisting heart attachments to our princess would give him a leg up in the "warm fuzzies" category. That happened to us. It was not on the list of prerequisites, but in a scenario only God could envision, Chris came with roots to Crossroads. He came to us from a thirteen-year stint in Las Vegas. The first contact was an email enquiry from Chris asking me for potential churches looking for a senior pastor within a one hundred mile radius of Kokomo. He assumed I had several years left in my tenure and had no idea my eyes were open to God's next man for us. I quickly discovered he had been gone from Kokomo for twenty years, but raised in our community through high school. Finally, we realized his grandfather had pastored our church for several years over half a century before he had sent his email. His mother had grown up in our church. Heart connections like those certainly helped in a situation like ours where the relationship between the pastor and the people ran so deep.

You would tell your daughters to do exactly the same thing before they zero in on any potential prince. The future of your church and successor demands that same clear-minded step, before the emotional vulnerabilities generated by charisma kick in. Do the hard work: develop a list of the attributes of a successor that you know the healthy future of your church demands.

FINDING OUR PRINCE

A search to find the prince in the absence of time pressures is a wonderful luxury. You give God maximum flexibility in the methods He can use to make the connection when you stay aware that the new prince could come from any place at any time. You're less vulnerable to mistakes when your finger isn't on the panic button.

Bill Hybels found a prince in Gene Apple at a kitchen sink. I found Chris Duncan in a buried email. You may hear your prince from another platform or hear about his strengths in a conversation about his success in areas of your core values. You can't rule out the ministry equivalent of Internet matchmaking, but God help you if you don't look beyond the lists of the unemployed, underemployed, or disgruntled.

You may have restraints imposed on your search parameters by reason of denominational requirements or financial limitations; but if not, then remember how much of the earth is the Lord's (1 Corinthians 10:26). There's no reason to think God doesn't have access to the perfect match.

CONFIRMING OUR PRINCE

Because I knew what I was looking for, it didn't take long for the telltale characteristics to catch my eye when Chris popped up. I knew from the first contact that: Family was important to him; he was acquainted with our community's culture; he had experience in leading a large staff; he was experienced speaking in front of large crowds; and he was committed to long-term ministry. Chris also had experience with a plethora of ministries to kids and aligned with our theology of worship and the weekend approach to it. In addition, I was now aware of the remarkable connection Chris had to our church I have already mentioned.

My first impressions were in place, but I wasn't the one who was going to have to live with him. I needed to create a pathway for Chris to our church's heart. I needed a plan that would help me confirm what I already felt, build consensus with my staff and lay leaders, and build credibility with the process and for the candidate before presenting him and the transition plan to the congregation.

The process Crossroads used to confirm my successor may seem over the top, but the first two steps we took flowed naturally out of my belief that the home is the sweet spot to gauge the princely characteristics of the candidate. You need look no further than the counsel I've already shared that Paul gave to Timothy when prepping him to look for a leader (1 Timothy 3:4-5).

In light of that verse, isn't it odd that we make our evaluations based on their visit to our home, rather than our visit to theirs? Doesn't it make sense that listening to him lead his kids in the kitchen is as important as listening to him preach to a crowd from the platform?

Let's look at the process in detail:

Confirm what you feel. After a number of phone conversations, it seemed obvious that the next steps should shift to a face-to-face discovery phase. Becky and I made a trip to Las Vegas, Nevada and stayed in

Chris' and Annette's home for three days and two nights. Over the course of the next three months, in addition to Becky and me, we sent two other envoys of staff families to spend time with Chris and Annette, in their home.

Build consensus with your staff and leadership team. Within two months, three more couples made the trip, including two young staff leaders and their wives, as well as my twenty-five-year administrative pastor and his wife. They spent at least three days and two nights in Chris' home to get acquainted and to watch Chris and his wife interact as a family in their own environment.

This gave us the perfect opportunity to measure our core criteria in a real life setting. What we accomplished with these two steps gave us the platform to introduce Chris and Annette as people we had worked at getting to know.

Build credibility with the confirmation process and for the candidate before presenting him and the transition plan to the congregation. I wanted to demonstrate that we had done our due diligence before recommending Chris to the congregation. After those visits, I was able to tell our congregation that staff leadership had been in the Duncan home for a total of ten days and seven nights. We had watched them interact as a family and were confident they had a healthy home. We also felt as good about Annette as we did about Chris.

I was able to tell them the values we esteemed for family, husband-wife relationships, and parent-child relationships looked fully aligned in the Duncan home with the model we held for all our people.

We were able to tell the congregation that we got to watch Chris walk through his church in Las Vegas as he introduced us to the staff of

Canyon Ridge. We were able to see custodial staff greet Chris in the same jovial manner as the lead team. We observed the whistle and bouncy step we came to love in the hallways of Crossroads when we were on the campus of Canyon Ridge. I was also able to report that the two younger staff couples felt as good about Chris as the older couples did (my wife and I included). Besides me, those three couples became Chris' PR agents in Kokomo.

From servers at tables in restaurants, to church attendees walking in the mall on the weekend, we watched Chris interact outside of the church environment. He left me standing more than once just to greet a large family and several 20-somethings hanging out at the mall. I was happy to report this to our congregation, knowing how important these components were to our body life.

I was able to tell them how Chris responded to a personal struggle I was enduring back home. Crossroads was navigating the toughest waters of my ministry. I suffered through more than one long phone call in which I received updates on the situation. I appreciated the sensitivity he showed and the input he gave to me. It was a side of his capacity to care that I was grateful to see.

Finally, I relayed how candid Chris was about his personal circumstances. He was frank with his past and personal demons. He was clear with his answers to my questions regarding theology and philosophy of ministry. I left believing I had gone several layers deep into the who of Chris and Annette Duncan.

HOW DID IT WORK?

The process worked like a dream. I got my confirmation through the staff members that made their own trip to the Duncan's. We gained credibility when we talked to the congregation about our recommendation for them to invite Chris and Annette to Crossroads as a next step. My staff felt included. The result was that we gave Chris an opportunity to win their hearts on his own.

You have to know who you're looking for before you see him. And you have to have a process to confirm that he's not just tall, dark, and handsome. It's work, and there are a lot of ways to do it. But I wouldn't mark one checkpoint off the list without figuring out how to authenticate his score.

Now, some five years later, I can tell you that what we found to be true in Chris' home in Las Vegas has proven to be true in his home in Indiana. You really can find Prince Charming for your Cinderella and feel comfortable throughout the engagement.

The most important resource you have in finding Prince Charming is The Prince of Heaven — the real groom of this beautiful bride. He has more than a vested interest. This choice is really His to make and ours to discover. He will not leave you alone in the process.

Be bold in asking. Be persistent in asking. Settle for nothing less than a sense of direction from the True Match Maker.

He has more than an opinion. He formed Cinderella's foot, He designed the slipper to fit the foot, and He will prompt the right prince to slip that slipper onto her foot. Jesus wants to make sure you don't miss him.

TIME TO REFLECT

. . . .

1) What does tall, dark, and handsome in a Prince Charming look like to you?

2) How would you put the search team together, and who would make the leadership team in your search?

3) Where are your hunting grounds for a Prince Charming?

4) What check or double check systems do you have in place to confirm a candidate and build credibility before his earliest introduction to Cinderella?

5) What role does your congregation play in choosing or confirming the successor to the senior pastor?

PART 2

THE CHOREOGRAPHY OF

A HEALTHY TRANSITION PLAN

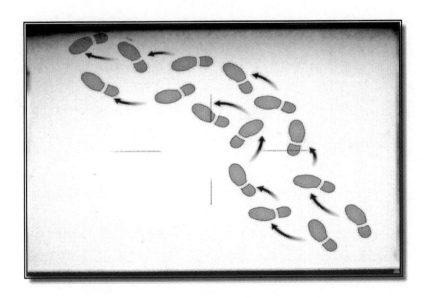

CHAPTER 6

. . . .

GETTING OWNERSHIP OF THE DECISION

> *Most discussions of decision making assume that only senior executives make decisions or that only senior executives' decisions matter. This is a dangerous mistake.*
>
> — PETER DRUCKER

Few commodities are more precious than unity. In the church, it is incalculable. Ask leaders to lead without it and you will make their job exponentially more difficult.

If you've ever had the privilege to lead with unity, then you understand what it means to be firing on all cylinders and moving forward with maximum power. If you've ever had to lead without it, then you, my friend, understand what it means to herd cats. If you've had it and lost it, then you understand what it means to grieve loss and undermine your goals. If you've had someone else lose it for you, then you understand the meaning of livid.

THE PARADOX OF UNITY: YOU HAVE TO FIGHT FOR IT

A comprehensive study of Paul's letters in the New Testament confirms his call for unity in the church. Paul urges each congregation and every leader to safeguard a spirit of oneness. One of the most powerful examples is in his letter to the Ephesians. Paul writes, "Make every effort to keep the unity of the Spirit through the bond of peace" (Ephesians 4:3).

Paul's choice of words when talking to the Ephesians about unity is starkly revealing. The English translation of the Greek word *spoudazo* in the NIV is "make every effort." The word means to struggle and strain, with a sense of urgency. Paul tells them unity is not manufactured on our part: it is maintained. To make sure they understand the importance of being on the same page, Paul uses the strongest of words to tell them unity is worth fighting for. Furthermore, the word implies the need for immediate and ongoing action with its sense "to make haste" in doing it.

If ever unity is a necessity, it is a prerequisite to leading a healthy transition. As odd as it sounds, fight for it if you have to.

I spared nothing throughout my pastorate in pursuit of Paul's injunction to the church at Ephesus. Unity is never more important to possess than during the transition season. I wanted Chris to succeed as the next leader of the Crossroads' mission with every fiber of my soul. I knew that could happen only in the environment of the precious gift of unity, which the Holy Spirit had woven into the fabric of Crossroads' culture. This fight was not a fight of fisticuffs, but of careful strategy, unwavering follow through, and relentless pursuit.

I grew up in a church that didn't guard its unity. Consequently, I also grew up in a church that spent too much energy trying to recover from the brokenness of dissension, and never getting far out of survival mode. Our team at Crossroads understood the priority of unity and our commitment to guard it.

The environment into which Chris would set foot was mostly up to me. The two of us would orchestrate the environment in which he would take his first steps as the senior pastor. If we couldn't make it happen together, it was doubtful he could make it happen when he was on his own. We were going to be champions for unity.

STRAP ON YOUR LEADER'S HAT

By this point, I could hear the orchestra warming up for the father-daughter dance, but I also needed to help the leadership team and congregation hear and understand what was happening, too. I had also navigated the first waves of my emotions about the leadership transition; now I had to help the congregation face theirs. I was convinced I knew who Prince Charming was. I had to help our leadership team and church body see that the matchmaker was Jesus and this match was heaven-made. Cinderella would never wander into these precious realities; we would have to lead her there. The process demanded my strongest leadership in the few weeks and months leading up to Chris's arrival. You'll have to strap on your leader's hat as well.

Leading a healthy transition demands that you gain ownership of the decision by Cinderella herself. Let's face it, if Cinderella ain't happy, ain't nobody happy!

You may be the de facto CEO, a member of the senior leadership team, an elder, or the senior pastor of a congregational church polity. Whatever the case, to grant legitimate leadership authority to your successor you have to gain ownership of the decision from the people. In our world, leadership is conferred by those who are led.

At some point in my leadership career, I decided to make voting my friend. I used votes to gain ownership and measure buy-in, not just grab permission. Every leader should wake up and smell the coffee: Keeping a ballot out of the congregation's hands doesn't restrict them from casting one. You know without me telling you that people vote with their feet, their hearts, their hands, and their pocketbooks. If you don't have the people's approval of the new leader, you're fighting a battle you will not win. A power play at this point will put the very team and stakeholders you love and appreciate at risk, as well as jeopardizing the very mission you're working to extend beyond your tenure.

I was never afraid of a church vote. Give me a demonstrably right decision and enough time and I would get more than a consensus decision. I went after a mandate and usually got it. I believed that if I couldn't lead a group of people in owning the decision, then I surely wasn't going to get them very far down the road to the desired outcome. I assigned lost votes to poor leadership, not obstinate subordinates. If the vision was sound, then my job was simply to help them see it before they got there. If they didn't see it, then that was on me.

Frankly, I enjoyed the challenge of leading voters to a mandate. Though it's not the same as leading the mission itself, it is precisely the same as casting the vision, with an immediate eye exam at the end to test their sight.

Gaining consensus was never more precious for me than the experience of getting solidarity from our most senior members to change both our location and our name with the same move. It was one of the trickiest steps in our dance. As with all tricky steps, it came with both high risk and high reward.

We had committed to relocate our campus and expand our facilities. A third strategic step was necessary to take our transformation to another level.

We were getting ready to move down the road. We'd reached an agreement on the property, but the title work had not started. I sensed some time earlier that changing our name would help us in our branding as a church, but had said nothing except to the most senior leaders. Because of the long-term implications, I knew it would be best if changing our name coincided with the financing and title work.

We planted the seed thought as we introduced the concept of a cafe in the former facilities. We strategically called it Crossroads Cafe. Before we started work on the blueprints for the new facility, the cafe had established both its value and identity as a nonnegotiable in the new facilities.

Before we left our old campus, I wanted to celebrate what God had done through the people of that little congregation. I invited the surviving twenty-seven members of the original crowd of fifty or sixty to lunch at a banquet room in one of our nicest restaurants. Some of them had been babies when we started; now they had families of their own. Others were single again after saying goodbye to a precious spouse who was already in heaven. They had a place in my heart reserved for no one else. Along with the much-deserved accolades for their faithfulness, I wanted them to know first, and get their permission, to change our name.

We spent time telling stories that made us both laugh and cry. I honored them for being people who became convinced that God was doing something special through them. I celebrated a maturity level that enabled them to think beyond themselves and perceive God's heart for reaching our community. It was at the core of their willingness to move from a location with so many precious memories.

Then I shifted the subject to the most delicate. In the past, Becky and I had announced her pregnancy for each of our kids. Those who were sitting in that room either grew up with them or helped to raise them. Now they were going to share in the biggest transition of our life: the marriage of our oldest daughter.

I took on a very serious posture and shared a story of a Harlow family crisis. "After Curt had asked me for Leslie's hand, he later made some comment about her changing her last name to Raab. It's a good thing he didn't mention that in the first conversation! I knew she was moving out of the house and getting on with her life, but change her name, too? But down deep I knew that changing her name would be less confusing and in the best interests of her family, so I conceded." I leaned forward and whispered to this little group who counted us as extended family, "But we know Leslie will always be a Harlow at heart!"

Before the chuckles subsided, I told them about another possible name change. "You know we're moving out of Oakford and down the road to the corner. It seems like it would be less confusing and would better serve our people if we changed our name to Crossroads. God has raised us up out of this community, and then called us to serve this community. That seems to suggest we would be better tagged as a community church." I landed the plane with the request, "With your permission, I would like for us to change our name for this new chapter of our life to Crossroads Community Church." Before they could catch their breath, I leaned forward once again and whispered, "But we know we will always be Oakford Baptist Church at heart!"

It gave rise to one of the most precious moments in my ministry. One by one, they either stood to their feet with tears rolling down their cheeks, or hugged my neck on the way out, each whispering their affirmation, "Jeff, it's the obvious, and it's the right thing to do." To the person, they cast their vote to make the change.

Like any strong leader, I used the decision as leverage with naysayers. It was rare to have mavericks or renegades on the team, and likewise in the congregation, but reference to popular referendums like these quieted any remonstrance to a murmur.

In an earlier chapter, I told you about the process by which I received personal confirmation of my successor and started gaining leadership collateral for stakeholder buy-in. Once those three trips were finished, and all the team members and their spouses (AKA assigned scouts) compared notes, we took a straw vote and knew we were on solid ground. Now we had the footing to take the next steps.

GET EVERYONE ON THE SAME PAGE

Have you ever made the mistake of reading the wrong scripture verse when speaking, while noting the right reference? Or reading the right scripture verse while preaching, but posting the wrong verses on the screens? You know something isn't working in the former; everyone knows it in the latter. Trying to lead a church in transition without everyone on the same page is like a conductor directing an orchestra when the musicians are not playing from the same score. It isn't pretty. You have to get every-one on the same page.

The rest of the team and stakeholders had to catch up with me in the process of this transition. Never forget that because you are the leader you got a head start and are comfortable with the proposed outcome. Be patient and give people the time you've enjoyed to process the steps you are getting ready to ask them to take.

John C. Maxwell hammers this principle home in his book, *Developing the Leader Within You.* "A good idea becomes great when the people are ready," he writes. "The individual who is impatient with people will be defective in leadership. The evidence of strength lies not in streaking ahead, but in adapting your stride to the slower pace of others while not forfeiting your lead. If we run too far ahead, we lose our power to influence."

Your stakeholders have to hear the music for the approaching dance for themselves. Help them understand what they are hearing, as well as the critical nature of the song. Ensuring clarity will never be more important than during a transition of leadership.

Your stakeholders have to get over the emotions of the impending transition. They will likely feel some of the same negative emotions you had. Don't lead like a dictator who ignores their emotions or be a general who barks orders; be a shepherd who leads them to quiet waters and helps them process those emotions. Share the positive aspects that helped you move beyond your negative emotions.

It is important to note that the leaders who spent time with Chris and Annette in Las Vegas had the permission of the whole leadership team to go. By setting up those visits, I had already started the aforementioned steps of transferring ownership of the decision to my staff and the deacon team. I needed them to help me lead. They needed their own time to process. It was invaluable in the momentum of this transition because it set the ball in motion.

After sharing with the team and congregation (in appropriate sequence and settings) that my role in God's mission for Crossroads was ending, I told them of my interactions with Chris Duncan. I let them know that there had been strategic steps taken to that point to get confirmation of Chris's compatibility with Crossroads. I shared the steps that we took and the reports that the team had given.

GET EVERYONE ON THE SAME ITINERARY

People travel better when they know where they are going and how they are going to get there. Getting your leadership team and the princess to the wedding on time requires an itinerary: a schedule of the points of interest and their planned times of arrival.

Gaining ownership of a decision demands a disciplined strategy. We put together a sound strategy covering the scope and sequence of the entire period leading to the day Chris Duncan would take over Jeff Harlow's office. I outlined the process that would fully engage the congregation in the decision to make Chris Duncan my successor and their new leader. Each step had its objectives.

Give the princess her own discovery time early in the process. We invited Chris to spend a weekend with us corporately, as well as spend scheduled time with various leadership teams, including an open forum for individual members to gain an additional level of acquaintance.

We set a short period of discovery for the stakeholders to ask any and all questions. My door was open and I attempted to address all concerns with integrity. We encouraged the leadership team and deacons to engage the members and become liaisons in the process. The significance of their role was predicated on the success of helping the support team own the decision themselves.

Lead the princess to the dance with baby steps and a safety net. Parents do not measure the length of the steps of their toddler before they clap for encouragement. And it is instinctual for dads and moms to hold their hands out to their little ones who are taking their first steps; not to guide them, but to provide a sense of safety as they take their first risky steps. Good leadership understands the steps you are asking many of your congregation to take is as unnerving to them as the first steps are to a toddler. Give them baby steps to take and a sense of security as they take them.

After the discovery period, we outlined a process that would include three votes:

First Vote. The congregation would take the first vote immediately after the visit to invite Chris to join the Crossroads staff. He would serve as the pastor to Next Generation Families, a position designed to begin building relationships with the young families he would be pastoring for years to come. We took the vote with an understanding that he was on a provisional path to become the future senior pastor of Crossroads.

Second Vote. The congregation would take a second vote six months after Chris's initial hire. This vote was to make the transition to the senior pastor position official. He would not be the pastor with this vote; his identity as the pastor to Next Generation Families would continue. It did not include the guarantee of final approval with this vote. But it was the official engagement of Prince Charming to Cinderella, if you will.

Third Vote. The congregation would take a third vote three years into Chris' hire as pastor to Next Generation Families. This vote was to invite Chris to become the senior pastor of Crossroads with a specified start date determined. We would set the wedding date.

We were not trying to be redundant with three votes. Each subsequent vote was another definitive step in the transitional process. We were acknowledging the need for equilibrium as the stakeholders took these steps, and these steps would provide the time and experience they required. Three votes gave them a safety net. We effectively lowered their risk with each vote. Each vote had its purpose. Each vote had its own set of perspectives.

As a report, each vote resulted in similar 97 percent affirmations. To let you know, though we tabulated them separately, at Crossroads we invite both members and nonmembers to vote on any congregational issues. This critical vote would be no different in that we invited anyone who felt as if he or she had a vested interest in the future of Crossroads to vote. We do, and did, ask them to delineate their status. Both categories of voters were materially the same in the final tallies.

Here's why we took three votes:

We based the first vote on the leadership collateral of the entire leadership team. As would be expected as the senior leader, my influence carried the most weight, but it was an invaluable comfort for them to learn of the three trips to Las Vegas. They needed confirmation as much as the leadership team did. Hearing the role that the rest of the team was playing gave integrity to the process. Hearing that we had spent extended time in his environment paid huge dividends. It was a key component to their willingness to trust the process.

The second vote was the most crucial. This one was all on Chris. We will talk in a later chapter about the personal focus I set and maintained during the three years, but my instructions to Chris were to get to know the people. I am a very relationship-oriented pastor. Chris is a very personable man. His biggest challenge was going to be in proving he cared about Cinderella as much as her daddy did. I wanted him to focus on getting to know the current staff, which he did. I wanted him to focus on getting to know the lay leadership, which he did. I had a very healthy relationship with them. Crossroads was stronger because they were serving. The lay leaders needed to develop a relationship of their own with Chris, and they did.

I also wanted Chris to get to know the leaders in making. I wanted him to spend time with the next generation. Hence, that's why we wanted him to lead Next Generation Families. They were the long-term leaders of Crossroads. This was the perfect opportunity to cast the vision and invite them to engage at another level. He did that as well.

He had to work hard, but the second vote was the crucial one, because he had to win their hearts to win their vote on his own. He did that, too.

The third vote would be no more than decorum. It actually served its purpose as a safety net while taking the second vote. It was the only slam-dunk of the three. By this time, there were some formalities left and some happy moments to celebrate, but in reality, we were at the end of this dance before we officially got there and counted the votes.

Once again, the final tally, interestingly enough, was the same. With the exception of the emotional realization of its finality, Crossroads was ready for Chris to show his stuff and lead them into the future, while being out from under any shadow I could not help but cast. And I'm happy to report that he did that, too.

Ninety-seven percent of those voting in a church of three thousand people said yes. I was happy with the final count. I was the happiest because I knew they fully owned the decision.

The strategy for helping Cinderella fall in love with Prince Charming was set in motion. Now what was I going to do? To be honest, my plate got more, rather than less full. It became all the more necessary for me to identify my responsibilities and focus my attention on transitioning leadership from me to Chris and to make the transition as healthy as possible.

The music to the final song had begun. Cinderella and I had three years left to dance. I wanted every step to count.

TIME TO REFLECT

. . . .

1) On a scale of 1-10, one being a hostile mess and 10 being a healthy ant colony, how would you rank the unity of your church? If your rating is lower than you like, what practical steps can you take to recover the unity that Ephesians 4:3 promises?

2) What, if any, are the challenges the congregation will face in accepting a candidate for a new senior leader?

3) What are the steps you could take to gain the endorsement of your leadership team and the acceptance by your congregation of a new senior pastor at your church?

4) What strategy do you have to familiarize your congregation with your successor after he gains entry to a position to win their hearts?

5) What would be the optimum time lapse of the transition process with the congregation from his introduction to installation?

CHAPTER 7

DEFINING YOUR OBJECTIVES FOR A HEALTHY TRANSITION

Setting a goal is not the main thing.
It is deciding how you will go about
achieving it and staying with that plan.

– TOM LANDRY

When you want to lead a healthy transition, defining your role in a fluid process is more important than most people realize. You need to set the agenda for your remaining days as the leader. And make no mistake: you're still exactly that. How you lead through the end will have everything to do with how your successor can lead from the beginning.

Law Number 17 of John C. Maxwell's book, *21 Irrefutable Laws of Leadership*, is "The Law of Priorities." He teaches, "Busyness does not equal productivity. Activity is not necessarily accomplishment. Prioritizing requires leaders to continually think ahead, to know what's important, to see how everything relates to the overall vision."

When you're still sitting in the big office behind the big desk in the big chair, transition will prove whether you're a leader by assignment or a leader at heart.

YOU MUST CHOOSE HOW YOU DANCE IN THIS TRANSITION

I had served as the pastor of Crossroads for 12,500 days before Chris walked through the doors for work his first day. I knew it wasn't just another day. I still had over three years' worth of mornings ahead of me as the senior pastor. A question struck me: Since the circumstances had changed, did my agenda need to? How was I going to lead through this last dance?

YOU CAN COAST

I could putter around for the next three years, doing a number of small tasks and not concentrate on anything in particular as I slid into retirement. After all, Chris was now in place and I could delegate the workload to the new guy. Even if you're tired, that option is as unreasonable as it sounds if you love Cinderella. Hurried transitions are harried ones for the princess, but they are better than transitions made interminable because dad is sulking, or has already checked out.

Leaders aren't coasters by nature, but doing so may never be more tempting than during your last dance. I couldn't coast if I wanted to. Even if I could, I was unwilling to make the church pay the piper for me to draw a paycheck, get in the way of someone willing to lead, and let the church wander without a leader for three years.

This is one of those cases in which all you have to do is read the option out loud and you would be embarrassed to give it a second thought.

YOU CAN MAINTAIN THE STATUS QUO

You are the senior pastor and you could simply function as such through the last day of your tenure. You have weekends for which to pre-pare, teams to lead, and meetings to attend. You would have no problem staying busy.

I knew I could stay busy until the last goodbye doing exactly what I had done for the previous 35 years. It had kept me more than busy B.C. (Before Chris), and my plate would stay full A.C. (After Chris). God had used that agenda to grow a church, and someone needed to preach funerals, officiate weddings, keep track of the sheep, and reach out to visitors to the end of my tenure. I didn't let those responsibilities slip, but I did make some significant adjustments on my priority list. I had to determine what Crossroads most needed to ensure a smooth transition to Chris as the leader and generate the maximum moment when the moment came. It was still business, but not business as usual.

YOU CAN LEAD THROUGH THE HANDOFF

When we see what God has purposed for us, we call it vision. Vision drives the agenda of good leaders. One of the biggest challenges for an outgoing leader is to find a visionary focus that allows for a healthy tran-sition. The question is, how does your role in a future that doesn't include you affect your immediate priorities? Find the answer in what you want to be true about Cinderella and for Prince Charming's first Monday after you're gone.

I chose to lead all the way through the handoff to the prince. I got a handle on what God wanted to be true about the future of Crossroads the first day without me. We'd settled on Cinderella's identity. Everything I did in the last few years of my leadership needed to revolve around her in order to secure the best environment for her and for Prince Charming as they started their new life together. The dad in me wanted my daughters and their husbands to live life at the level to which God had purposed it for them. The pastor in me wanted the exact same thing for Crossroads and Chris.

A MISSION WORTHY OF YOUR LAST DANCE

That deep desire for Crossroads to live up to her potential and God's purpose after she danced into the arms of Chris helped me clarify my objectives for the last three years of leading. Three qualities had to be true for that to happen for Crossroads, and they are just as necessary for your church. Focusing on these qualities will dictate a mission worthy of your last dance with Cinderella. They provided the grid to determine all I would and wouldn't do during the transition.

CINDERELLA'S IDENTITY IN GOD'S EYES

One of the ironies of the original Cinderella tale is that Cinderella herself did not recognize who she was and how much she meant to the prince or to the story. After the party, she was all but ready to settle back into a life of drudgery and remain confined to the classic definition of a Cinderella — a person of unrecognized merit or disregarded beauty.

On the shortlist of preconditions for a healthy transition is for your church to have a robust understanding of its identity. This serves as your true north. A church has to go into a leadership transition segue knowing who she is and why she exists. You can navigate the uncharted if your compass always reads true north.

Identifying Crossroads' identity required us to talk about our mission, values, and vision. I had three years to make all three clearer than they had ever been.

Rehearse your church's mission statement. Your mission statement serves as the explanation for everything you do and the catalyst for asking what you are not doing, but need to do. It is the point of the needle of the compass as you navigate the uncharted waters of change. You must be committed to chiseling both the words and the meaning of your mission statement into the soul of every serious member of your church.

If you know why you exist, you can relax when new leaders rollout emerging strategies to accomplish it. The how can evolve when you have a firm handle on the why.

Few conversations are more important with your successor than making sure his compass points the same direction as the church's. At Crossroads, our mission statement is, "Meeting people where they are and helping them take their next step with Christ." I needed to know if Chris just thought our mission statement was cute, something he could make himself live with, or serve as the purpose that would define his tenure as Crossroads' leader. He convinced me in the earliest conversations that it was consistent with his call, and would frame his life and energize his ministry at Crossroads. You need the same assurance from a suitor for your princess.

Reinforce your church's values. Your church's identity doesn't rest singularly in her mission statement; it is birthed out of your values, which, in turn, gives rise to her vision.

You must be committed to reinforcing your church's values: the ideals that you esteem as a church. They are what you believe, no matter what. They are the hills you would fight on and, if necessary, die on. They are foundational to who you are.

In John W. Gardner's book, *On Leadership*, he wrote, "Every healthy society celebrates its values. They are expressed in art, in song, in ritual. They are stated explicitly in historical documents, in ceremonial speeches, in textbooks. They are reflected in stories told around the campfire, in God-moments kept alive by old folks, in the narratives told to children."

We had opened the newest Crossroads' facility with a sermon series on our values, "This Must Be a Place." I felt led to the same title for my final series. Our values were just as core as I was finishing my preaching career at Crossroads as they were the day we changed our name to Crossroads and opened a new facility. I wanted them to be the last words they would hear me speak. In that season of transition, the operative question was, "What should change and what should never change?"

I prepped the congregation at the beginning of the series for its climax. We invited the entire congregation to "write in stone" the one core value they believed must never change. I purchased tons of beautiful western river rocks, cleaned them, and then laid them out across the steps of our large stage. At the conclusion of all four services that weekend, I summoned every member of the congregation to the front with a permanent marker in hand to write in their own handwriting, "This must be a place of _____," and then had them sign the bottom. It was a moving experience to see the seats empty and a sea of people move forward to make their declarations.

The people of Crossroads inscribed 2,000 river rocks that weekend as an affidavit consigning future generations to the core values of our church. They made declarations such as, "This must be a place of worship," "This must be a place of Truth," "This must be a place of healing," and "This must be a place of connections." To read what the people wrote was one of the most satisfying experiences of my ministry. They really got it.

The stones will create a beautiful wall feature around and over the large entryway to the auditorium. Those rocks will cry out as a cloud of witnesses to everyone who enters and exits: "Never forget and never let these values lose their currency."

While strategies, programming, teaching methods, environments, technology, and curriculum may change throughout the years, your core values must remain the same. Write them in the proverbial concrete and etch them in their hearts. Better yet, get those core values written on a wall of rocks in the personal handwriting of real people. Those names, when noted, and those declarations, when read, will serve as a battle cry to their descendants for generations.

You must find a way to clarify your core values and transfer them into the future to ensure they transcend leadership transitions.

Recast your church's vision. When your values drive you, you can't help but discover your vision. For example, the core values of the centrality of kids, the role of the family, and the supportive role of the church drove the Crossroads vision to be a church of homes based on the model described in Deuteronomy 6. Moses wrote, "Hear, O Israel: The Lord our God, the Lord is one. 5 Love the Lord your God with all your heart and with all your soul and with all your strength. 6 These commandments that I give you today are to be upon your hearts. 7 Impress them on your children. Talk about them when you sit at home and when you walk along the road, when you lie down and when you getup. 8 Tie them as symbols on your hands and bind them on your foreheads. 9 Write them on the doorframes of your houses and on your gates" Deut. 6:4-9).

We have become committed to assisting parents and grandparents in the spiritual development of their kids. We are certain that an hour a week is not enough to shape the faith of a child; it takes the other 167 hours in the home.

We used rocks again to serve as lasting reminders of their personal commitments to the vision. We asked them to find their own rocks and bring them to a designated weekend service. We invited them to step from their seats as families, gather as a household at the front of the auditorium, and write their declaration of commitment on their rocks: "We are a D6 Home."

They dated it, took it home, and placed it in a prominent place to serve as a reminder of their vow.

We used the three years of the transitional process to recast the key components of Crossroads' vision. You can use bumper stickers, wall art, or engraved boulders along your driveways, but find ways to recast your vision. Successfully clarifying your church's identity will serve as purpose enough to energize your remaining tenure, but maximizing your church's health to secure the living out of your vision is mission critical before you leave.

MAXIMIZE CINDERELLA'S HEALTH

You must be honest about the health of your church as you think about the maximum potential of her future under anyone's leadership, particularly your successor's leadership. You want your church to thrive, not just survive.

When recently asked, "How would you define a healthy church?" my one-word answer was alignment. I'm not a chiropractor, but I understand the debilitating effects of misalignment on the body. You don't have to be a chiropractor either to recognize the impact of misalignment in your church.

Please don't misunderstand me, or dismiss the importance of this consideration if your church is not driving with handicap plates or close to its last rites. Crossroads was a strong church, and yours may be as well. Like Crossroads, you can have ministries that are strengthening people's faith, shaping families' home lives, and serving your community's needs. But both our churches will underachieve if we have misalignment issues.

There were four areas of alignment to which I believed Crossroads had symptomatic problems: staff solidarity, programming to mission, small groups, and finances. Your list is as unique as your church, but two of those are so critical that they deserve our consideration here.

Staff solidarity. Turf wars among church staff are like autoimmune diseases that produce antibodies that work against the body. They rob your church of energy at the least; they will knock the life out of your ministry at worst. Of all that will be on the plate of your successor, don't hand him an unhealthy team.

The game changes when your attention to staff alignment succeeds and you see them connecting at the heart and not just at the table. The synergy that comes from working together is very powerful — so much more powerful than if they are acting as mavericks who are running suc-cessful, but isolated programs.

Mavericks believe they are working for the common good, but are inadvertently hurting it.

I was unaware of a single relational issue on our staff. We didn't dislike each other, but we also didn't connect at a level conducive to maxi-mum health. Trust builds relationships, and trust provides margin of error and benefit of the doubt in seasons of vulnerability. Though solidarity existed in pockets, we had never succeeded in making it a safe place to share our hearts and lock our souls together as one. We were missing the synergy of the whole being more than the sum of its parts. That had to change.

We made two critical hires, and we almost overlooked them both. These guys turned out not only to be good at what they did and fun to be around in a personal sense, but they also sought ways to help other ministries succeed. Those two men led the rest of the staff in forgetting about turf and hierarchy, making available anything they had to help another team member succeed. The connections crossed workplace etiquette and the component parts of Crossroads ministries began to work in sync, not just in the same space.

We picked up momentum with each phase of the three-year transition as the staff came into alignment with the big picture. You could sense the energy building.

Programming to mission. Healthy transitions demand you submit to programming alignment evaluation, adjustment, and rehab. None of it is fun, but it is fundamental to health. The ramifications of physical misalignment range from pain to paralysis. The consequences of programming misalignment in the church are no different.

It was sometimes too easy to say that Crossroads was "meeting people where they were." We had a propensity to forget to evaluate how we were helping them take their next step. The former was not a standalone proposition.

More consequential than that were concerns that ministries didn't know why their programming was working or not working. I wanted people to understand why we did what we did, as well as why it worked.

For a time, my younger staff took offense at my insistence that they defend their positions. When I asked, "Tell me why . . ." in that season of staff alignment, I didn't want to irritate them, but I was determined to make them understand the theorem before they could use the rule. I wanted them to be able to replicate what they were doing. I wanted them to be able to strategically evaluate and adjust their approaches.

BUILD AN EFFECTIVE PLATFORM FOR PRINCE CHARMING

Get the prince on the weekend preaching schedule. When talking with a leadership team of another church going through transition, they asked if I thought a new senior pastor could lead as part of a team teaching system.

"Yes, I believe in the team teaching approach," I said. "But, no, I don't think he can do it if he's not the primary teacher on the team."

If that was to be true after I left, then it had to be true while I was leaving, so we started with the weekend preaching schedule. If we had begun with a softer start that gave Chris more time before the second vote, I might have paced it differently. But because we had the crucial second vote within six months, Chris and I nearly split the speaking responsibilities from the beginning of the transition.

Give the prince leadership responsibilities. You have to see the prince's capacity to lead leaders. Can he conduct meetings and keep focused? Can he encourage leaders to fulfill the vision? It is also wise to see how he works with the personalities you have on staff. And it gives the current staff an indication as to their fit with the prince's style.

Once a month we had a lunch meeting for all of our full-and part-time staff, as well as with key lay leaders. Chris set the agenda and led the meeting. I wanted our leaders to get a sense of Chris's style and become comfortable with him setting the tone.

Give the prince legitimate leadership responsibly. You have to see the prince's capacity to lead teams and their ministries. Can he cast a vision for the future? Can he generate momentum? Can he make adjustments to improve effectiveness? How does he resolve conflict in a struggle? How does he use the whole team to accomplish the mission?

Chris became the staff representative on our Preserve Marriage ministry team. Crossroads is highly vested in ministry to marriages. We dedicated ten acres of beautiful woods, $750,000 in facilities, and a full-time staff member committed to developing healthy marriages. It had also been at the center of the most damaging leadership blunder in the history of Crossroads, with a renegade staff member leading the debacle. To delegate that position to Chris was a huge risk, but it was a focus dear to his heart. He took it, and we made great strides under his leadership.

Give the prince freedom to roam. Healthy leadership transitions are a matter of building trust. Chris had to be free to caucus with key people if he was to have full leadership momentum on his first Monday morning. We gave him that freedom.

Chris had to trust both Crossroads and me for him to leave a good situation at his previous position at Canyon Ridge, move his family nearly 2,000 miles, and risk that one shot in the prime years of his life in Kokomo, Indiana. He had to trust that I was actually stepping away from leadership. And he had to trust Crossroads to shift its loyalties and follow his lead after I stepped aside.

Crossroads had to trust that the Holy Spirit led its instincts, that Chris was the right person to succeed me, and that he could be their pastor.

We had to trust Chris to commit to long-term ministry and not just use us as a stepping-stone in his career to some self-serving pinnacle.

I had to trust Chris. I had to trust him to let me lead through to the end of my tenure and feel good about finishing well. And I had to trust him behind closed doors with me on the other side of that closed door! If he was a visionary, he couldn't help but see potential initiatives consistent with our mission long before he was in the best position to lead in taking steps to make them happen. I couldn't expect, let alone want, him to stuff his dreams of Crossroads' future. He had to be free to dream and cast vision from the first day after I stepped away.

Informal clusters gathering around Chris to brainstorm about the future derails nothing and should cause absolutely no consternation, but I must prepare you that it still feels a little weird when you see it happening. But mark this in your notes and watch for it to happen: When the leadership transition occurs at the functional level, it is the earliest sign of a new reality.

Put the prince in smaller settings with the princess. One of my all-time favorite quotes from John Maxwell is his axiom written in *Developing the Leaders Around You.* He contends, "You can impress people at a distance, but you can only impact them up close."

That very principle moved our Father in heaven to send His Son to earth. Jesus came to give His life as a ransom for our sins (Matthew 20:28), but He also came to not only show us who the Father really is, but how He really feels, and what He will do in a relationship with us. The author of Hebrews wanted believers who were going through a time of struggle to know that "The Son (Jesus) is the radiance of God's glory and the exact representation of his being" (Hebrews 1:3). Jesus came to get closer to us.

Getting your successor in front of people is important, but preaching and leading meetings alone will not give him all the leadership collateral he will need to help Cinderella fully relax when thinking about the future. You want people to do more than just listen to him: you want them to follow him. It's best to build that level of trust in smaller settings.

Nothing we did during the transition process had greater impact in winning the hearts of people to Chris than what we called our "ReThink Possible Initiative." Though ReThink was a strategy implemented to clarify the Crossroads vision and increase the personal ownership of it, another value emerged in the process. The biggest win was getting Chris and me into small settings, watching us play off of each other, and hearing his heart for the vision of Crossroads.

The logistics involved a five-week blitz that included getting Chris and me into home settings with ten to fifteen Crossroads attendees for a fast-paced hour of vision casting.

Chris and I were candid about the challenges Crossroads was experiencing in problematic areas, and shared specific courses of action we were initiating to address the issues. We defined what it meant to own the Crossroads vision in terms of attendance, giving, and serving. We used a powerful tool to help them gauge their personal ownership of the vision, and then challenged them to take at least one step deeper in their level of ownership.

"ReThink" was the most effective and personally rewarding method to cast vision I used in my entire ministry. We were able to speak to over one thousand individuals representing nearly six hundred homes in small groups that included interactive dialogue. Whereas any previous effort to meet with the church body in small settings attracted only the most committed, we went deep into the demographics of people living on the fringes of Crossroads' life. People we had never connected to the Crossroads mission came out of the shadows and gathered with us in home settings. The impact was dramatic and in the months that followed, we implemented every initiative we presented. But nothing superseded the connections it initiated at the personal level between Chris and the people as they got a small setting exposure to his heart.

In addition to the steps I've just outlined, I made it a strategic point to refer to Chris from the platform as often as appropriate. I'm not sure there was a measureable rate of increase as time went, but certainly a conscious effort from the beginning. I also referred to him in the majority of my church communications, such as letters and emails.

Factors vary from one circumstance to another in the transition process, but you can't rush a healthy transition. Crossroads allotted nearly three and a half years, and we needed every one of them. You might have less time, or even need less time, but don't cheat the three objectives I have outlined. Preexisting relationships of the prince and princess can reduce the time requirements, such as serving in a support staff position, but make no mistake, it's still a transition.

The climactic moment of a father giving his daughter to her prince is at the end of a road we call engagement. That same kind of moment when one leader hands the pastoral care of a church over to a new leader lies at the end of a road we call transition. But for both sets of circumstances, you can get a feel for how this is going long before you get there. Let me assure you as one with experience: define your objectives and relentlessly pursue them and you will find yourself during that climactic moment of finality feeling good about it.

TIME TO REFLECT

. . . .

1) What objectives should make your to-do list during the last dance of your tenure?

2) On a scale of 1-10 for each subject – values, vision, and mission – with 1 being blissful ignorance and 10 being able to articulate the subject, where would you rank your church?

3) On the same scale, where would you rank your congregation's understanding of the correlation between the values, vision, and mission of the church now? At what point on the scale could you see your congregation by the time you exit? What steps could you take to help your congregation move up that scale in each area?

4) On the same scale, when thinking about your church's health, with 1 being on life support, and 10 being practical alignment, where would you rank the alignment of your programming to your values, vision, mission, and staff solidarity?

5) What score in each of the above areas would you feel good about as you exit? What steps could be taken to move both your alignment of programming and your staff solidarity from where it is to where you want it to be?

CHAPTER 8

DEALING WITH DOUBT

> *In faith there is enough light for those who want to believe and enough shadows to blind those who don't.*
>
> — BLAISE PASCAL

Doubt finds its way into our lives in lots of disguises. Whether it's as innocuous as second-guessing, as embarrassing as insecurity, or unnerving as confusion; doubt will happen in some form or fashion, whether you expect it or not. My moments were short and random. I suspect doubts can be more frequent and challenging to answer while still falling into the category of doubt, rather than all out catastrophic breakdown.

Billy Graham, the nation's pastor for three generations, takes the edge of chagrin out of the quandary with the observation, "Doubts are a normal part of life. We doubt things on earth, so it's easy to doubt things of God" (*Dealing with Doubt*).

WHEN YOU GET SCARED, RUN HARD IN THE RIGHT DIRECTION

Sometimes circumstances do not make sense, or you discover idiosyncrasies that had previously gone undetected. Maybe it's been a bad day for both Cinderella and Prince Charming, causing the wrong kind of sparks to fly. Maybe the princess or the prince has become a little hypersensitive or they're not cutting each other enough slack. I don't care who you are; the Bible prepares us for circumstances exactly like this when Paul reminds us, "Now we see things imperfectly as in a cloudy mirror…" (1 Corinthians 13:12, NLT). Don't be surprised when you get surprised.

I chuckled at the account of an interview with an African safari guide who was asked, "Is it true that jungle animals won't harm you if you carry a torch?"

"That depends on how fast you carry it," the guide said. So, is it true that doubts won't harm you if you have enough light? It depends on how you run. It's not a question of if you have doubt; the question is what you do with your doubts when they jump out of the jungle shadows. When you catch yourself running, make sure you run hard in the right direction.

Tim Keller, author, speaker, and the founding pastor of Redeemer Presbyterian Church in New York City, New York, and author of the book, *The Reason for God: Belief in an Age of Skepticism*, puts the embarrassment of doubts to bed. Keller writes, "A faith without some doubts is like a human body without any antibodies in it. People who blithely go through life too busy or indifferent to ask hard questions about why they believe as they do will find themselves defenseless against either the experience of tragedy or the probing questions of a smart skeptic. A person's faith can collapse almost overnight if she has failed over the years to listen patiently to her own doubts, which should only be discarded after long reflection."

The cautions of Dr. Keller will serve us well when the winds of doubt pick up. Doubts can whip against the fundamentals of our faith in God or our confidence in a transitioning successor working through the process of a solid plan. Whatever those winds measure on the anemometer of doubts, and wherever those winds hit as we walk by faith, how we deal with our doubts is the issue.

You may even encounter those days Max Lucado calls "doubtstorms: turbulent days when the enemy is too big, the task too great, the future too bleak, and the answers too few" (from his book, *In the Eye of the Storm*). Never more important than then, you have to deal with the facts and fight against emotion winning the day. Doubtstorms demand methodical processing in the same way disquieting thoughts do.

SOME SECOND GUESSING THAT'S HARD TO BELIEVE

The most astonishing account of doubt in the Bible came toward the end of a long awaited, masterfully planned, and seemingly seamless leadership transition. And it makes the shortlist of most critical transitions in God's plan to redeem humankind.

What makes this account most extraordinary is that it was the reigning CEO of the faith world at the time, John the Baptist, who experienced those doubts. Father God chose him to announce to the world that the Bridegroom was in the house. Jesus chose him to share the intimate privilege of baptizing Him. And John heard the very voice of the Father affirm His Son while still in the baptismal waters, followed by seeing the Holy Spirit descend from heaven in the tangible form of a dove and alighting on Jesus. How much evidence should a guy need that this was the Prince Charming?

John the Baptist was so sure His Holy Successor had shown up to take both his place and God's plan to the next level that he turned to the crowds with his booming voice and declared, "It is the bridegroom who marries the bride, and the best man is simply glad to stand with him and hear his vows. Therefore, I am filled with joy at his success. He must become greater and greater, and I must become less and less" (John 3:29-30, NLT).

But then comes those shocks to the system, hard times that catch you off guard. John finds himself in a dark, stifling dungeon that was little more than a pit in no man's land. After some eighteen months in the limelight, this free spirit of the wilderness was confined and isolated in prison for probably as long as a year.

John began to doubt Jesus' identity as the Christ. However long he struggled internally, he could contain his second-guessing no longer and took steps to get his question resolved. Matthew records John sending word by one of his friends to ask Jesus, "Are you the Messiah we've been expecting, or should we keep looking for someone else?" (Matthew 11:3, NLT).

Jesus stood up for John in the midst of his doubts and in front of a crowd that was surprised by the prophet's quiver. Whereas John likely expressed his doubts with no more than a whisper, Jesus raises His voice so loudly we can still hear it today, "Were you looking for a prophet? Yes, and he is more than a prophet. John is the man to whom the Scriptures refer when they say, 'Look, I am sending my messenger ahead of you, and he will prepare your way before you.' I tell you the truth, of all who have ever lived, none is greater than John the Baptist" (Matthew 11:9-11, NLT). Jesus was neither angry, nor disappointed in His battle-worn friend; He simply answered John's doubts.

Whatever finally qualifies as faith, I agree with Dr. Martyn Lloyd-

Jones who said, "Faith is the refusal to panic." Even in the middle of his most perplexing moment, John refused to panic. He acknowledged his doubts and went to the only One who could assuage them.

Well, I was happy to have Chris on the team, but he wasn't Jesus and I wasn't John the Baptist. So there was no surprise when those flashes of doubt cast a shadow on my confidence. I've not asked Chris, but I don't have to. You can bet Prince Chris had some second-guessing of his own creep up.

WHEN CAUGHT SECOND GUESSING, FOLLOW THE RULES OF DOUBT-BUSTING

I always hoped to hear a question in my own head before I heard it with my ears. When it's my question first, I have time to process the answer when hesitation doesn't fuel someone else's doubt. Admittedly, sometimes people have the gift of doubting and beat me to the punch. Even then, you have to follow the rules of addressing doubt, as I've listed below.

Don't Worry Alone. When doubt takes the form of worry, John Ortberg Jr. offers this remedy in his book, *The Me I Want to Be: Becoming God's Best Version of You.* Ortberg writes, "Never worry alone. When anxiety grabs my mind, it is self-perpetuating. Worrisome thoughts reproduce faster than rabbits, so one of the most powerful ways to stop the spiral of worry is simply to disclose my worry to a friend . . . The simple act of reassurance from another human being [becomes] a tool of the Spirit to cast out fear — because peace and fear are both contagious."

Matthew's account of the dark period in John's life includes the detail that he shared his doubts with his closest friends, and asked them to help him sort it out.

Admittedly, the circle must be small, and the counsel must come from trusted friends, but don't do this by yourself. I tell people, "Asking questions, even of God, isn't a problem; it's supplying the answer yourself that gets you in trouble."

I have, at minimum, that small circle which includes my wife and my prayer partner. Depending on the area in question, I also have a well-beaten path to a select group of confidants.

Who would make that list for you?

Let the plan work. Unless you're working on a whim, you've already established your plan. Let it work.

The safety net of three strategic and sequential votes cast by vested stakeholders, covering three years, calmed most of my involuntary tics. When you're playing the role of the therapist, encourage your doubting friend to do the same.

Andy Stanley, pastor of North Point Community Church in Alpharetta, Georgia, described this same rule with the statement, "Consider your doubts and carry them with you. It's not a reason to abandon the plan."

In the case of Jesus' disciples doubting Christ as their prince, Stanley reminded his people of the final decision they made during a particularly unsettling time. When the crowds were changing their minds and taking off, Jesus cast a glance toward those closest to Him and asked, "So what are you thinking?" To paraphrase Peter as he became the voice of reason: "Who else gives us a better chance of giving us what we're looking for?" (John 6:68).

It's a clarifying question to ask when you're struggling with your heir apparent: "If not him, then who in the world would it be, and where in the world is he?"

The disciples didn't get all of their questions answered during that disquieting season, but they kept moving forward and they carried their doubts with them. They had settled on a plan and they let it work.

Remember what you already know. Rabbi Berel Wein, an American-born Orthodox rabbi, lecturer, and writer, declares, "A people that has no memory has a most difficult and uncertain future as well." He followed up by saying, "One of the basic requirements of Judaism is the gift of memory. The Hebrew word *zachor* — remember — is key to many of the basic mitzvas and values of Judaism" (*Jewish World Review*, March 10, 2006).

Paul tells believers that a healthy memory is key to stability in faith. In Romans 5, after acknowledging we go through seasons of life-squeezing pressure, he reminds us that it produces character. I like the KJV translation of the Greek to English with the word "experience" in verse four. Paul writes, "Therefore being justified by faith, we have peace with God through our Lord Jesus Christ: By whom also we have access by faith into this grace wherein we stand, and rejoice in hope of the glory of God. And not only so, but we glory in tribulations also: knowing that tribulation worketh patience; and patience, experience; and experience, hope: And hope maketh not ashamed" (emphasis mine; Romans 5:1-5, KJV).

The Greek word translated as "experience" in verse four puts the emphasis on the potential positive effects of repetitive pressure. Over time, it produces character. The use of the word "experience" in the KJV puts the emphasis on the been-there-done-that effect of repeated struggles.

When a similar struggle comes up, your response becomes a

calming memory that solidifies both process and outcome. You tell yourself, I know what I did the last time this happened, and it all worked out in the end. I'm going to do the exact same thing I did and believe it will get me the same results. My personal paraphrase of Paul's conclusion in verses four and five is, "That type of response always builds hope, and hope never disappoints."

When the winds of doubt would pick up during our leadership transition, I would remind myself of that first email from Chris, the first phone conversation we had, the three trips to Las Vegas, the first vote taken by the congregation, etc. The body of evidence reminded me of why I had felt so confident.

Keep a journal of the mile-markers that confirmed your position on this journey. Let it work like the history tab in your web browser. Spending time remembering what you already know will go a long way to lay the winds of doubt to rest.

Keep struggles in perspective. Jesus never answered John's doubts with a simple, "Hey, John, it's me, Jesus! I know you were there at my baptism, but let me say it again. Yes, I'm the right guy!" No, a paraphrase of Matthew 11:4-5 says Jesus simply pointed to what he was doing beyond John's personal dungeon: "What I told you I would do, I'm doing."

I read a fascinating article written by Alina Tugend that The New York Times published on March 23, 2012, entitled "Praise Is Fleeting, but Brickbats We Recall." Tugend quoted Clifford Nass, a professor of communication at Stanford University:

"The brain handles positive and negative information in different hemispheres," said Professor Nass. "Negative emotions generally involve more thinking, and the information is processed more thoroughly than positive ones," he said. "Thus, we tend to ruminate more about unpleasant events — and use stronger words to describe them — than happy ones."

I think Professor Nass is correct. We tend to overreact to negative information. The article goes on to advise the reader of how to effectively deal with difficult circumstances that call for negative feedback and reporting. If you're trying to improve a person's productivity or quality of work, you must be aware of how you sequence the subjects you address. If you give all of the positive feedback in preparation for the negative, by the time you finish with the negative, the individual has forgotten your positive input. Human resources experts suggest addressing negative issues first, and then stabilize the person with positive feedback.

The perpetual demands of leadership as a pastor tests every person. Given enough time, those tests will reveal every area of strength, as well as discover every facet that needs refinement in the most promising leader. Chris made his mistakes and had his *faux pas*. Any person you bring in as a potential successor will have his own.

I received occasional reports and made personal observations of ruffled feathers and rough edges that needed refinement in Chris' interactions with our people. But there was never a stretch of time without positive feedback about the evident gifts and strengths that my promising successor brought to the table. Chris made every week and weekend better as he led teams, spoke from the platform, and connected with people. Crossroads was connecting with Chris.

Address the issues that arise and ask questions the transition process sparks, but don't let them blind you to the signs that demonstrate he has what it takes to do what the job demands. And whatever you do, don't let the last word be the negative one.

Keep looking ahead. "Where there is no vision, the people are unrestrained" (Proverbs 29:18, NASB). The imagery of this verse is vivid: where you lose sight of the future and God's plans and instructions for it, people run wild. There is no direction, and there are no boundaries. Losing the vision that moved you from the beginning creates an exposure to unwarranted second-guessing that leads to unnecessary vulnerability and unsettling double-mindedness.

You simply can't afford to stop looking forward. The old Roman philosopher Seneca said, "To the person who does not know where he wants to go there is no favorable wind." Norman Vincent Peale said, "No matter how dark things seem to be or actually are, raise your sights and see the possibilities — always see them, for they're always there."

If in those rare moments of wavering during the transition, I could have taken a breath of the fresh air I've been breathing since Chris replaced me, it would have instantly swept away every concern I had. I was able to end well. I am enjoying the happiest year of my life since the transition was completed. The church has flourished under Chris's leadership. There are new families in the seats and new hands sharing the reins. The finances are stronger than any time in our history. Crossroads is taking missional steps down paths I never even considered.

You are a leader. You've recognized what God has started, you won't be able to finish. You are demonstrating your capacity for vision by simply pursuing input as you make a leadership transition in your church. If your successor had to give a state of the union message the first weekend after he assumed the senior pastor position, what do you want him to be able to say about the condition of the church? If he outlined the agenda of the church for the next year in that same talk, what values do you want to shape his thinking? How can you make Prince Charming's first Monday in the office a happy day after you're gone?

Take the time and write it all down. Keep it close and pull it out when the winds of doubt begin to pressure your soul.

Whatever the source of your doubts and whenever they hit, always answer them. Don't dismiss them as embarrassing thoughts or let them fester as an unwelcome antigen. Though your doubts might turn out to have substance, it's still best to address them head on. Just as the body develops immunity to overcome harmful viruses or bacteria, once you identify the unsettling pathogen in the transition process and develop the proper anti-bodies to neutralize it, you can thrive in an outbreak of doubt.

TIME TO REFLECT

. . . .

1) How did your parents deal with seasons of doubt?

2) Are you naturally vulnerable to doubt? If so, why?

3) How do you normally deal with doubt?

4) Who would make your list of confidants in times of doubt?

5) Make a list of the mile-markers that served to confirm the choice of your successor.

CHAPTER 9

. . . .

LEADING THROUGH TO THE END

> *Even if you're on the right track,*
> *you'll get run over if you just sit there.*
>
> — WILL ROGERS

A question you need to answer will get further details a little later, but stick this question under your hat: What do you do when the chairs move and you're close to the end of your tenure?

Sometimes chaos just happens and you realize the prince issued orders while you are still in charge of the house. This chapter is not about wearing your stars so everyone, including your successor, can see them. It's about leading the healthy transition you want all the way to the end.

WHEN THE WHITE WATER HITS THE FAN

One of the items on my bucket list for retirement was a 240-mile rafting trip down the Colorado River through the Grand Canyon. After I handed the reins to Chris, I took the trip and it was one of the most thrilling experiences of my life, made happiest by sharing it with my son, Will.

Between the starting point at Lee's Ferry and the ending at Lake

Mead, the Colorado falls almost two thousand vertical feet. Nearly half of that drop takes place inside roughly 160 pockets of white water whose linear distance, when added together, amounts to less than ten percent of the canyon's length.

Detailed only as one who has experienced it, writer Kevin Fedarko in his book, *The Emerald Mile*, describes this topography as "a pool-and-drop phenomenon, [which] means that the river is composed of long stretches of tranquility punctuated by intervals of unholy chaos."

Throughout the entire rafting trip down the Colorado, I caught myself seeing parallels to the ministry I had just finished. Both rides were longer than I could imagine at the beginning. The beauty of God's work in creating the canyon and the beauty of what He created at Crossroads moved me. Each trip had seasons of majesty, weariness, calmness, and chaos.

Every bend of the canyon and pulse of the river was breathtaking. But the analogy of white water on a powerful river in a beautiful canyon is perfect for the principle of this chapter. It's as true in the chaos of the church as it is in the chaos of the water on a river: You must lead through to the end, not just to the beginning of the end.

Sometimes Cinderella and the guests get confused as to who's guiding the rafting party to the takeout point. Neither you nor the prince can afford that confusion in those chaotic moments. And your relationship, based on mutual love for Cinderella and reciprocal respect for each other, must be healthy enough to work your dories through rougher waters and coordinate your actions based on your individual roles.

As always, leading is not just a function of being in the front of a moving line. You have to know where you're going, where you are in relation to those intervals of unholy chaos, and what actions are required in the anomalies of each feature (not all white water is created equal).

Martin Litton is a primary character in *The Emerald Mile*. He is not only a decorated World War II pilot in the U.S. Glider Corps, but also, and more importantly in this story, a champion conservationist and the most revered guide on the Colorado.

Fedarko says that mixed with Litton's good attributes (the ones that made him the consummate guide) were some negative ones:

[Litton had] an incorrigible habit of taking his eye off the ball, as he was often likely to be in the midst of yet another instructional lecture or anecdote, rather than paying attention to the river. Thus he'd be caught completely unaware — pointing out some feature of the canyon, building to the punch line of a long story, or concentrating on lighting up a cigar — while merrily drifting downstream with his back to an upcoming rapid. When one of the passengers gently inquired about the jet-engine roar emanating from around the bend just ahead, he would spring to action, ordering life jackets fastened, drinks put away, hatch lids slammed down and battened, all the while looking for a dry space to stow his cigar.

As you can imagine, not every story that started this way ended happily.

WHITE WATER IN THE OFFICE COMMONS

You can't lead a healthy transition by simply enjoying the scenery and drifting unaware toward potential chaos. Somebody's going to get wet, hurt, or worse. Let me give you an example of a situation that could have gone very wrong if I hadn't led through to the end.

I overheard (certainly the operative word, seeing that I was not privy to the party) bits and pieces of casual conversation of an upcoming furniture move in the office commons. This was, admittedly, not a *coup d'état*, but it was more than somebody who might say, "Honey, I'm bored with the furniture arrangement in this room." This was a reassignment of the usage for the area.

The plan involved moving furniture out of the most beautiful space in our entire facility, overlooking our small lake out front. It also boasted a manmade creek, delightfully streaming from its base down to the main body of water. The midsize, open room included my favorite tables and complementary chairs, leather couches and chairs, and a gas log fireplace.

I had come to refer to it as "The Commons." It was the eye-catching focal point of every visitor who entered the office complex, and a hub of weekday activity, both official and casual. It became the favorite haunt of staff members, meeting places by teams, and groups of lay-led Bible studies. It was a type of family room for our church leadership.

Remember that one of my three objectives during the transition was to maximize church health, which included more than the staff, but the staff was at the core of it. I noted that objective with an admission: Though I knew of no friction in that season of staff relations, we weren't buzzing with warm and fuzzies. I believed that needed to change.

The Commons was just across the staging area from my office. It sounds like an overstatement, but it was like seeing friends on the porch swing when the staff sat casually around those tables or on the leather furniture. I knew they were often doing their own work, which could have been, and historically was, done in their personal office pod. But a sense of community existed out there, which drew people to do their work there. It radiated the sights and emitted the sounds of people who enjoyed being together. And I loved seeing and hearing them. Most importantly, it was more than just a barometer of staff health; it was an engine room for it.

I understood precisely why Chris was about to commandeer it. It was the perfect setting for the hour or two a week that he would spend telling the Crossroads story and casting vision to potential members. I was simply confident that the area could be reconfigured for Sunday mornings and kept functional for the aforementioned purpose and practical usages for the other 166 hours a week.

After I overheard of the potential room revamp, but before the actual makeover took place, I thought I'd nipped the move in the bud with indirect conversations. But rather than talking directly to Chris, it could well have been that I used one of my oft-doomed approaches of leading: either I would leak word back through the chain or simply drop some hints that would hopefully catalyze common sense. One of my incorrigible habits is that I believe others ought to understand me when I leave sufficient clues. This seems like a reasonable approach to mentoring, but it rarely seems to work.

Having thought I had sufficiently delayed it until the prince was leading, if not killed in caucus, the waves pounded me before I heard the roar of white water. I walked into the office one day, and that beautiful room had taken on two of the features of the house described in Matthew 12:44: "swept clean" and "empty." It had been stripped barren of everything except a single small table with four chairs. My heart still palpitates with the flashback of that memory.

So, what do you do when your staff moves the chairs and you're close to the end of your tenure? Like establishing an action plan in any emergency, you plot a course of action with your successor that allows you to address issues in a moment of crisis without a meltdown.

RULES OF ENGAGEMENT
WHEN THE WHITE WATER HITS

STAY CALM

Nuclear meltdowns are never good, particularly at a late date in the transition. If it's mishandled, it can do some serious damage to a healthy transition. Even when caught in unexpected white water, when clear heads prevail, the worst that can happen is typically no more than a good drenching. If you've gone into it with life vests pulled snug and helmets strapped tight, then even a good dumping runs its course into quieter waters. It doesn't have to escalate into anything more than a chapter in a book after it's all over.

GAIN CLARITY

Back to *The Emerald Mile*, I love Fedarko's description of Litton when he knew they were on the cusp of turbulence. He writes, "In the midst of this frenzy, he would stand up to take stock of where they were, then turn to face the line of boats behind him and issue instructions about the name of the rapid and what needed to be done."

My first mission was to find and invite Chris to my office. As I recall, I successfully refrained from using an envoy or email. Direct is best, unless you think the person needs to sweat, a tactic appropriate for a repeat offender, but not for a first timer.

I understand the impact of environment on a conversation. It was in my office. We ran into each other in the staging area. (We might have crossed paths in The Commons, but the kitchen table was gone!) I didn't say anything on the other side of my office door, nor did the meeting commence until the door was shut. Like fussing parents, I think that kids recognize when there's some tension in the air, but I didn't want any public humiliation in what was just a course correction.

I stood while he sat. I wanted to exercise the authority that was still mine in that moment, but I wasn't going to talk down to him. We talked eye-to-eye with the implication that this was a single-agenda meeting.

IN THE RIGHT DIRECTION

White water is no time for timidity with the oars. You must stroke strongly and in the right direction. Strong strokes in the wrong direction will only magnify the coming deluge. That direction may seem counterintuitive to some, but you're the one with the oars in hand, it's your boat, and it's not your first rodeo. It's chaos and your call, so make it.

Our conversation began with a clarification that this healthy transition was going to stay on course and that we were still on schedule for him to become senior leader at the point already determined to be beyond that moment. It was a recitation of established protocol for significant adjustments and a clarification on the definition of "significant."

A TEACHING MOMENT

It became a teaching moment to help Chris understand that this was not simply a breach of protocol, or an inadvertent crossing of leadership lines: there was rhyme to my reason for wanting that room to stay as it was. I wanted him to know the role I believed it played in our community life. I wanted him to know the impact on visitors as they walked in, not just seeing the view, but seeing staff interacting.

I also wanted to tell him that I thought his new approach to casting vision and welcoming new members was excellent and that this was undoubtedly a great place to conduct it. I wanted him to see I could have my cake and he could eat his, too. We could turn this room over every weekend.

A FINAL DECISION

Finally, I told him it wasn't happening on my watch; if he wanted to mess this place up after I was gone, he was free to do it. (No, I didn't say that. Actually, it didn't come to mind until I got to this point on this list.)

Reinstalling the furniture and reinstating its original intent was the right call for that room before the water really hit the fan. Follow through must be quick, obvious, and commensurate to the issue.

As I remember, Chris and/or the staff returned the furniture before the end of that day. Though Chris had delegated the furniture's removal, I think he participated in its restoration.

LEAVE IT BEHIND

Chris and I never talked about this issue again, and I'm not telling anyone else but you. We never will, unless he reads this book! Chris may well forget all about it until he's the dad and the Prince Charming of his transition shows up. Then I wouldn't be surprised to hear he is having a flashback as some white water hits him in the face.

I got on Chris' nerves sometimes, and he got on mine, but I don't remember another incident like this one. I'm more grateful than I can say that the transition was healthy and we hardly experienced a sniffle.

I liked Chris from the beginning, learned to love him quickly after we met, and love him more than I can say today. He was about to take the people I loved on the next leg of their spiritual journey and to the next level of God's plans for Crossroads. I not only wanted him to be okay with me sticking around during an extended engagement, but I also wanted him to be glad I was there all the way through the wedding. Never once did Chris disrespect me. As much as we teased each other, I was never the butt of his jokes.

I admit I wanted more than a good relationship and fun times. I wanted Chris to be all the better after I was gone because I had been with him for a while at the beginning.

It's not if, it's when the white water hits. And when you hit it, the crew and passengers may not have time to decide who has their ears. Get it settled and keep it clear before the jet-roar around the bend.

To the crowd, sometimes it may look like you both have the baton. And, quite frankly, that may well be true for the shortest of times. But make no mistake about it: it has to be yours until you both know it's his.

Lead all the way through to the end.

TIME TO REFLECT

. . . .

1) What is your definition of white water?

2) What are the biggest rapids in your church?

3) What was the biggest wave of white water to blast your boat during your tenure? Why?

4) How do you normally address conflict?

5) What do you believe is a healthy action plan to resolve conflict between the leadership team or you and your successor?

CHAPTER 10

REACHING BEYOND YOUR TIME

> *I alone cannot change the world,*
> *but I can cast a stone across the waters*
> *to create many ripples.*
>
> – MOTHER TERESA

If influence is about making ripples, then leadership is knowing where to cast the stone. Over the years, I had thrown plenty of stones to create ripples in order to raise money or catalyze collaboration, but this shortage of time was uncharted waters for me.

Time was now a factor. I had to cast my last stone toward a future to make waves in a season I would not play. I had some serious ripples to make, diminishing sand in the hourglass, and I only had one stone to throw. It had to be opportune and a dead on bull's-eye.

ONLY GOD

Nearly four decades before, I had registered a particular concern with God as a young pastor thinking about the risks of a growing church: "God, I don't know how I could ever help someone with the loss of a child." I knew then that day would come, and it did. And it came more times than I had prepared for in that moment. It happened again as I was on the verge of leaving.

This promising young family was sweet in spirit and sold out for the Lord, perfectly fitted for the Crossroads mission, and they were expecting a child. As Brady walked away from one of those special conversations that energize aging leaders, he turned and said, "Pastor, I'm so excited about our place in Crossroad's vision. And to top it off, in the morning we get to hear our baby's heartbeat for the first time!"

That next morning, Misty's nurse nervously excused herself, and the obstetrician quickly came in. After what seemed like an eternity of searching for sound with her stethoscope, the doctor broke the news that the heart of their little baby was not beating.

They placed one of their first calls to me. News of the couple's loss rocked my heart. They had already chosen a name for the boy: Hudson. The biblical dictum to mourn with those who mourn (Romans 12:15) must surely be one of permission, not a command. In circumstances like these, it is reflexive.

Then I realized that not only did this young couple have to bear the loss of their dear child, but also the cost of burying the only tangible remnant of his life. And I knew that the necessities of that process would not be cheap. My cry was instant to the One who always hears the cry of the heart: "God, it's too much! Do something." It was simple, but it was the expression of my overall confusion and frustration.

And then I heard that old, familiar Voice that I had come to recognize and cherish: "You can do something about this."

It was a short answer replete with understanding. I knew it was God and I knew exactly what He meant. I wanted God to do something, and He made it clear that He could do something, but He would be doing it through Crossroads. We couldn't bring Hudson back, but we could bear some of his parents' burden as they laid him in heaven's hands. We had the resources of fifty acres of land, a leader in the funeral home industry and connections in county government. God was leading us in how to use them.

This is no reflection on my successor or yours, but we are talking about leadership transition, not proxy implantation. You must establish in the discovery process of your successor the security of the values, mission, and vision. You want him leading from those secured principles, but you have to anticipate that fresh eyes may see different priorities and new perspectives that yield new strategies. Healthy transitions can't be achieved with anything less.

At the same time, we have just finished talking about leading through to the end. If you don't quit being who you are, then there may well be an inspirational moment that comes while time is expiring.

LOOKING FOR FIRE IN THE EYES

There simply wasn't time to get the project fully completed before I exited. I had six months, including the holidays, my farewell series, and the focus of the last goodbye weekend to do whatever I could and had to do. I threw everything I knew about leadership into that last initiative.

Before I created any waves, I needed to know if this was an emotional pipedream. So, I called my dear friend, Jeff Stout. He was the owner of the largest funeral home service in north central Indiana. His number was generally the first I dialed under heart-breaking circumstances like this one.

Out of a sense of personal propriety, it was protocol for Jeff to extend complimentary services to young families suffering such tragic loss.

My friend was in county government. His position would afford me the exact answer to my two-pronged question: "What would it take for Crossroads to establish a memorial garden to serve families sustaining the loss of a preborn?" And, "Would you help us do it?" Jeff's answer to the latter inquiry took less time than asking for it. He answered the former question with a bullet list of steps that couldn't be skipped, but, "Yes, it could be done."

My next step was to talk to Chris. I felt perfect freedom to share both the story and the vision for a memorial garden. I didn't have to sensitize his heart to the need in general, or to this young family in specific. But the flash that comes to the eye from the soul set on fire with an idea was not there. You had to be there with the family in the moment, when you had to search your own soul for answers. And you had to be there to hear the Shepherd tell you how to come alongside His sheep. I wasn't frustrated with the perfunctory response, but I was undeterred.

Step three was to go to my administrative pastor, Kevin Smith. Part of what made him so good at the role he had played for twenty-five years was his ability to manage the here and now. Kevin was outstanding in that role and I had kept him busy at it. I also recognized that his natural gifting didn't lend as quickly to creating momentum in the genesis moments of something new. I knew I would need Kevin before this was over, but I didn't expect the fire in his eyes right then either. I was right.

I still knew I needed leadership support to supply energy at the driving level. From my first dreams outside of the normal duties of pastoring, my deacon team had served as both a sounding board and a catalyzing encouragement. I needed them now, and I knew I could kindle some fire in their souls. I shared what I believed was one last directive to me from heaven, as well as the time limitations of my remaining tenure. This call was to them, as well as to me. I needed them to help me supply energy to the next wave of ripples. They didn't disappoint. The whole board was supportive, and the chairman stepped forward to join the official team that was tasked to lead the charge.

BUILDING AN ALTAR IN A CEMETERY

Then I took the big jump. Not that I needed to, but I burned the ships on the seashore. I told Brady and Misty the day before the memorial service that I had heard a Voice from heaven, and that God had heard theirs. He would use Hudson to change the landscape of Crossroads and the face of our ministry to the community.

I told them we were taking steps to create a ministry and memory garden to serve families sustaining the loss of a preborn. We would call it "Heaven's Hands" and it would offer a family a place for the little body of the life they loved, but never held. We would offer it to anyone who had the need and had heard of this place. It would include support during and after the services, and we would offer it free of charge.

I will never forget the spark of fire that came to their sad eyes. Like Elijah in the face of such a challenging moment, I saw the fire of heaven fall on the wet altar of their crushed hearts, and it set their spirits ablaze. In that moment, I had my champions for this vision. That fire spread to little Hudson's extended family as we stood by the grave that would hold his body until it joins every other at the resurrection. That circle of grandparents, uncles and aunts, and closest friends would become the first to help underwrite the capital needed to get the vision started.

The ripples needed more energy though to fuel the oscillation process necessary to generate the waves that had yet to reach the far banks of a working vision. And the clock was still ticking.

I had to articulate clearly the vision to an increasing number of people. This proverbial altar in a cemetery would give people a place to: weep; honor life; connect with their child, other mourners, God, heaven and eternity; be comforted at the deepest level; renew their hope; and begin to heal.

Making Heaven's Hands happen would necessitate connecting key people to the leadership team. I had my friend, Jeff, who understood the steps necessary to meet the legal requirements and zoning ordinances. He would lead the way to securing mandatory permits.

I talked with a prominent obstetrician in our church who, as only God could orchestrate, had previously spoken to another leader in our community about the desperate need for a ministry like this. She not only would join the team, but also play the role of liaison with our local hospitals. She would also serve to extend the welcome to other medical professionals.

The administrators of the local hospitals themselves opened the doors of partnership with this new initiative. Several doctors and nurses eagerly joined the movement to meet a need that had left them grasping for something tangible to help their patients after such a catastrophic loss.

I shared the new ministry from the platform one weekend. The ages of women who have suffered the loss of a preborn covered a wide spectrum of our adults. Women who had lost a little one four or more decades earlier came forward to join the team.

An article was published on the front page of the local newspaper about a kindred ministry Misty had initiated by making bracelets for grieving mothers as a keepsake and declaration that the life they carried was real and eternal (a ministry that has reached nationwide and beyond). The article included the description of Heaven's Hands, and it generated a huge response.

The base of Heaven's Hands was expanding and the energy to keep the ministry going was in full supply, and flowing to the point of need. A team that became a tightknit unit led it with a laser focus and personal passion.

The sand in the hourglass of my tenure was nearly gone, and so was I. Now was the time to ask my administrative pastor to step in. He did, and he did it as well as he always had done everything else I asked. He later confirmed what a joy it was to lead that sweet team.

Crossroads conceived Heaven's Hands in a challenging moment and birthed it nearly a year later as we stood on the beautiful hill dedicated to serve its purposes. The site provided easy access for grieving families, as well as to make a powerful declaration of the sanctity of life to thousands who drive by it. It took more time than I wished, but missional objectives usually do. They called me back to speak at the dedication as my first act of service since I had made my exit earlier that year. It was a powerful moment I will never forget.

Your exiting initiative may not be like Heaven's Hands, or even one of that proportion; but it certainly could be just as close to your heart and as core to the mission of your church. If you find yourself as I did, and the last verse of the song of your daddy-daughter dance is playing, there is a way to strategically throw a stone and create some meaningful waves beyond the reach of your tenure.

THE TWO-MINUTE DRILL
OF AN OUTGOING LEADER

SHARE THE IDEA

Dr. Martin Luther King Jr. lived to share his dream. The threat of death would not quiet him; the assassin's bullet didn't silence him either. Take King's advice: "Our lives begin to end the day we become silent about things that matter." Don't let your tenure end before your time does.

Take your first steps by sharing your idea with three different audiences. I would encourage you to disclose it first to your most trusted confidant, followed by talking with your successor, and then with key members of your leadership team.

READ THE RESPONSE

You may never be more vulnerable to just another idea than in the waning moments of your tenure, but we're still visionaries. Watch for the fire in the eyes of your successor. Maybe you can cast a vision he catches. Put comparable credence in the feedback of your leadership team. You're going to need those previous partners to carry on after you're gone. Your response to them should be consistent with your response to your successor.

CALCULATE THE TIME

Know your timetable. Be realistic about the calendar, both in agenda demands and initiative requirements to launch and secure sustainability of the idea. John Maxwell nails this one in his blog, *Leadership Wired*: "Passing On A Positive Legacy." John writes, "Leaders who have an enduring influence keep one eye on the compass and the other eye on the clock."

REASSESS YOUR POSITION

Wisdom will reward you if you ask yourself at least four questions:

• Is your idea consistent with the values, mission, and vision of your church?

• What is your motivation?

• Why must you do this now?

• How will you feel if this doesn't happen?

I would have counted it one of my greatest failures if Heaven's Hands had not become a functioning ministry. If your successor shares commensurate urgency for the initiative, let him do it. If moving the ball forward causes conflict, reconsider. If the proposal only makes his list of nice ideas, but you believe this must happen and happen now, then keep moving forward.

There does a come a point at which you shouldn't throw the stone. You may need to step away with the trust that God will move someone else to throw it and make the waves.

If you get to the point that you know this can and must happen, that it's time to burn the boats and not look back, then the next steps offer a process to follow. Along those lines, I love the adage Peter Drucker uses to admonish leaders, "The best way to predict the future is to create it" (Scripps Howard News Service).

FIND A CHAMPION

Though it's always a good idea, leading beyond your time demands that you find a champion. He may be a staff member or lay person, but find the person with the fire, both in the eyes and the belly, for the initiative. He's going to need it.

BUILD A TEAM

No one needs to tell you the value of team. You're not going to be there to keep them aligned with the project or, more importantly, with each other. Instead, identify a staff member who can develop a cohesive group and then support him or her.

BROADEN THE BASE

The more energy you can generate in making waves, the farther they will travel, the faster they will get there, and the more powerful they will be when they arrive. The broader you build the base, the more likely the success of the vision. Make your list of potential team members and cast the vision. Then share the vision with the church body. If the ministry connects to the community, then use the media.

MAKE IT OFFICIAL

As with the church, Heaven's Hands never missed a heartbeat with our staff leader transition. You don't have to live out your tenure as the proverbial lame duck. Mahatma Gandhi said it well: "You may never know what results come of your action, but if you do nothing there will be no result" (Forbes, "12 Great Quotes from Gandhi on His Birthday").

Paul is the most reliable encourager when you understand that he told the Galatians they should decide what they wanted to be true in the future, plant the right seeds, stay focused, and work the plan to the end (Galatians 6:7-9).

Concept became reality at Crossroads even though I was transitioning out. The ripples of that stone's throw crossed the chasm of leadership transition and will oscillate long after the navigation of future

Crossroads transitions.

TIME TO REFLECT

. . . .

1) Do you wrestle with the concern of becoming a lame duck leader? What areas are at risk if that fear becomes reality?

2) What steps can be taken with your team and your successor to safeguard against lame duck leadership before you leave?

3) Are there any significant initiatives already settled in your soul that need a stone to be strategically cast before you exit?

4) What are the steps you normally take to execute a plan that births a new program?

5) Who are the go-to people within your leadership circles who can help you energize an initiative while you're there, and lead within the framework of your successor's leadership team after you're gone?

CHAPTER 11

THE BLESSING

My father gave me the greatest gift anyone could give another person, he believed in me.

– JIM VALVANO

I think all dads would ban the song "Butterfly Kisses" from weddings. It's just not fair to us!

We had just finished the rehearsal for my oldest daughter Leslie's wedding. I missed the decision to play the "Curt and Leslie Video" before we went to dinner. I just heard the edict to sit down, so I settled into a seat in the front row of the auditorium, thinking I'd put the hard part of the evening behind me. Wrong.

When I realized the photos in this video were of my little girl when she was *really* little, and they were tracking her through the early years of life, it was nearly more than I could handle. But then I heard Bob Carlisle singing his song "Butterfly Kisses." He sang about the day he walked his little girl down the aisle and she changed her name. When he described one last butterfly kiss to dry his tears, it turned on mine! While trying to hold my composure, I heard this open whimper. I quickly realized it had come from me! In that moment, my goal for the next day was a lofty one: *Don't sob when you cry*!

That may sound a little dramatic when coming to this point of a leadership transition process, but you better brace yourself. We had been strategic and methodical in getting to this point. We understood what the season meant. This daddy pastor was as ready as Cinderella and Prince Charming. But that didn't mean I was going to be able to contain my emotions.

TURNING THE DAYS OF MINISTRY INTO MOMENTS OF MEMORY

This was about more than the ceremonial passing of the baton. We had enjoyed such a beautiful relationship that the church and I took most of my last month to celebrate. There has to be a way to say goodbye and express your love for each other. We found it, and so must you. You can't move forward in a healthy way unless you find a way to bring closure. There has to be a moment, and there was. And that's a good thing.

Walt Disney captured the heart of every kid when I was growing up because he understood how to create moments. He understood that whether we are thinking about 13,733 days of being the leader of a church, or the thirty days we spend celebrating them, it isn't the days in life we remember, but rather the moments.

CELEBRATE!

A pop song that made my personal teenage version of iPod is playing in my head as I think about this step in the daddy-daughter dance. How in the world the artists came up with their group name I don't remember, but they called themselves "Three Dog Night." Like lots of songs of the past, I can't recall the verses, but I can still remember the chorus stirring the emotions and rousing my generation to celebrate life and dance to the music!

Those aren't words from the wisdom guru who wrote Proverbs, but it does come from a page in the life of his dad, King David. There are times when you feel so happy and the little kid in you is taking over again. Let him dance! However long your tenure has been, you've got some things to celebrate, so do it.

Spend time together as a staff. Talk about sweet memories and funny stories. Talk about the people whose shoulders you stood on, as well as the more unique people whose antics you laughed at. Include the lay leaders as you celebrate. You would not have experienced the same level of success in your ministry without them, so give those key leaders a place at the tables of celebration. My staff had fun at the parties. They gave me a round of gag gifts, accompanied by light-hearted jabs at my "distinctive" qualities. They were fair, but they needed no cue cards to share — they knew me.

Don't forget to honor your spouse and the role she played in your ministry. The pastors' wives threw a retreat night to honor Becky. That group of ladies had met together for years to support and encourage one another. They were good friends. It was a night that Becky counts as special in the transition.

Gather around the table with your elder team. Our last deacons' meeting was a special time. Admittedly, they don't party with quite the frivolity as my still-maturing staff, but they had their fun with some stories only they knew (and what happens in deacons' meetings, stays in deacons' meetings). Then they did what they do best: they laid their hands on me and prayed. God put those godly counselors around you to serve an indispensable role. They will want to bless you. My deacon team did exactly that and it was a priceless moment.

Other teams who have helped to make ministry in your church happen will want to party with you. Make time to do it. You will also want to spend personal time with specific individuals who have shared the load with you over the years. Let the cameras flash and the food flow. Let them tell their stories. You and Cinderella have some serious goodbyes to say.

NO TOMORROW

As your church parties with you as the VIP, use the time to take full advantage to express your thanks for their camaraderie. Even after Paul moved on from his ministry in Thessalonica, a part of his heart stayed in that church and with those people. His next to last recorded ministry directly to them was to write a letter we call 1 Thessalonians. As he instructed those people he had once pastored, he couldn't help but express his thanks for them. He wrote, "We always thank God for all of you and pray for you constantly. As we pray to our God and Father about you, we think of your faithful work, your loving deeds, and the enduring hope you have because of our Lord Jesus Christ" (1 Thessalonians 1:2-3, NLT).

One notable regret I have is of a party that was mine to throw, but I didn't. I simply didn't think of it. I failed to get the alumni of the early seasons of Crossroads' history together as a group. We had so much to celebrate and express. I have such deep love for them and an equivalent sense of gratitude for the role they played from the beginning of my ministry. It was an inadvertent oversight on my part.

Though Crossroads seemed to be in a constant state of transition throughout my ministry, there certainly were some people God had used to bring stability and lay the foundation for what we became. I'm confident you have a similar list of people that come to mind. Don't overlook them.

I've heard a friend of mine say numerous times over the years that you need to dance with the ones who took you to the dance. He understood that you didn't get to where you are by yourself, so don't forget about those dear friends after you get there. After all, the people we are talking about are all part of the Cinderella with whom you are dancing. Those pioneers took us to our first dance; save a last dance for them.

ONE LAST PUSH

Paul gives us a beautiful example of giving people one last push before you leave. Paul and the people from the church at Ephesus wept as they embraced for the last time, but his purpose in getting them to the beach was to encourage them to continue what God had started. He admonished them to be careful, take care of each other, teach the Word of God, and to be givers rather than takers (Acts 20:17-36). It was a tender moment.

While my kids were still young, I heard the story of a dad who headed for the seat in the stands he had never left empty in order to watch his talented son run the last race of his stellar hurdling career. It was a seat that gave him a vantage point to watch him start, then attack and clear each hurdle as he moved down the course. But he chose his seat strategically to watch his son cross the finish line. He was high enough, yet close enough, to see the determination in his son's eyes and the strain of every muscle in his body.

Before the dad could reach his seat, his son waved him down to the starting line. Out of deepest respect and appreciation for his dad's faithful support, the champion hurdler honored his father with a request for his greatest fan to hold his starting blocks for his last race. Not only was it an offer of honor, it was an important position to fill. The offer was special and the answer was quick. You bet he would do it.

Dad got a view of his son that he had never noticed before: the tension, the twitching, the settling in, and the explosion of the start. It was a moment, one followed by an unobstructed view of his perfect handling of the first hurdle.

Then came the second hurdle; his son was still visible, but he was somewhat blocked from the details of the approach. Subconsciously he realized as the race progressed and the distance between them increased, that he would only be able to see his son as he jumped the hurdles; the dad would not even know that his son had cleared the previous hurdle until he saw him jump the next one.

Suddenly the thought hit this great athlete's father: For the first time in his son's career, he wouldn't be there to cheer as his boy crossed the line. He had helped his son start a race that he wouldn't watch him finish.

That's the seat in the house I had on that last weekend I spoke. I realized that this wonderful position I had filled over these years had moved to the starting blocks of the next race in Crossroads' journey. I had relished a front row seat to watch her rise to the occasion and cross the lines in victory for thirty-eight years. Now God had asked me to play a strategic role in my church's first steps in a race that wouldn't include me. I was in a perfect spot to watch her clear the earliest hurdles, but I was quickly coming to the point in which I would only see how she handled the obstacles in her continuing journey. And I knew she was running a race I wouldn't see her finish. It was a moment I can hardly think about even now.

It was my last daddy-daughter talk before Cinderella walked the aisle. It was my chance to clap for her. It was my chance to wonder at the "Peters" of Crossroads I had watched slip over the side of the boat and take legitimate steps on the churning waters that threatened the journey. It was my chance to marvel at the distance they were from the boat, more than measure the distance they were from Jesus. By using that tape measure, they were closer at the time of our last dance to being who God had called them to be and doing what God had called them to do than they had ever been before.

In those moments of wearing the pastor's mantle, I realized Cinderella was at a juncture similar to Peter's when he hung between faith and fear somewhere in the waters between his seat in the boat and where Jesus was on the water. And it was right then and there that I got to clap my hands and shout through the flood of emotions, "Cinderella! You're closer than you've ever been! You're doing this. Keep walking!"

I wanted to walk every hallway and stick my head in every classroom, clap my hands and say, "Staff, deacons, volunteers, leaders, and dads and moms, you're doing this! And you're so close to another level! It's within your reach! Keep walking!"

I hope I walked off that platform and out of the building on that day with every person God had entrusted into my care hearing the message in his or her soul: It's within your reach! Keep walking!

Evidently they did hear me, because they've kept walking. They're even farther from the boat and closer to Jesus in this day than they were in that one.

A MARKER TO REMEMBER

Becky and I wanted something tangible to give to express our heart for the faithfulness and friendship of the Crossroads family. You catch yourself agreeing with William Arthur Ward, author of the book, *Fountains of Faith*, who said, "Feeling gratitude and not expressing it is like wrapping a present and not giving it."

On our last trip to Israel, which we took the summer before our exit, Becky and I purchased 3,000 communion cups in Bethlehem. Those cups became the personal gifts to the church we so deeply loved. We wanted those olive wood cups to be more than a keepsake — Becky and I wanted them to serve as an invitation to adopt one of our family's most cherished D6 traditions: family Communion at Christmas and Easter.

Our family Communion is the most meaningful faith talk that I have with our grandkids. The intimate time we share around our table is an opportunity for Becky and me as Grandma and Grandpa to share our personal salvation story with our grandchildren. When our grandkids are saying their last goodbye to us, I want them to rest assured where Grandma and Grandpa are going, and how they are getting there. Becky's parents and my mom share their stories as well. Then each of our adult children shares their salvation experiences with their kids, as well as with their nieces and nephews as uncles and aunts. I want the kids to know the story of when, where, and how salvation happened for each member of their extended family. And I want the kids to know when their dad and mom accepted Jesus as their Savior. I want them to know the details that make it personal. Then the grandkids take their turn, including high-five moments for the kids who have accepted Jesus since we last celebrated the Lord's Supper.

Then, distributed by the dads and husbands, each person receives the bread and cup. The cup is the point. It's their cup, made of olive wood and purchased in Jerusalem, bearing their handwritten name and date of its first use. It's the cup they have used and will continue to use after Grandpa's and Grandma's chairs are empty. It's the cup that will remind our grandkids of the salvation story of each person who has left the circle and, most importantly, of the One who purchased their salvation.

The last service provided the opportunity for Becky and me to give them the cups. I rehearsed the family tradition as one last opportunity to press the core value of family faith talks into their souls. I wanted to give them the gift of a powerful tradition that kept on growing in worth. Becky and I also felt it wouldn't be bad if every time they thought about Jesus and their salvation while using the cups that they also had a brief thought of us!

The plan worked. It has reportedly catalyzed many families to adopt this tradition. And it has the capacity to remind them of our love for years to come.

Find a way to give them a gift that says thank you.

BLESS YOUR SUCCESSOR AND HIS FAMILY

My family wanted to give our public blessing to Chris and his family, so my staff arranged for the Harlow family to close each of the three services by praying a blessing over the Duncan family. Though the crowds were too large to get everyone within touching distance, we did ask each person to take at least one step toward the front as a personal act of faith and declaration. The sound of that movement was a powerful thing.

On Saturday night, Will, my oldest son, prayed for the two young daughters of Chris and Annette. Through his tears, he asked for God's blessing on them. He prayed that God would reward their sacrifice with joy, and that growing up as PKs would be as safe for them as it had been for him and his siblings. It was a prayer that made his father proud, their father hope, and the Father smile.

To conclude the first service Sunday morning, Becky prayed for Annette. Crossroads had enjoyed the best as a pastor's wife for the same number of days that they had me. Now it would be Annette's turn. What a sweet gift she is to Crossroads. I tell Chris we both married up.

Once again, we asked the entire congregation in attendance at that service to take at least one step toward the front. They packed out the large area in front of the platform, as well as all of the aisles of the auditorium. Then Becky prayed as only one pastor's wife could pray for another pastor's wife. Becky loved Annette. Annette had won her heart from the first moment we stepped into her home in Las Vegas some three and a half years earlier. It's not as though Annette lacked anything to do the job before that prayer, but when it was over, she knew she had Becky's blessing, and the strongest sense that she also had His. Finally, the moment came as we concluded the second service that Sunday morning. I had danced with Cinderella for the last time. Now the pastor was looking me in the eye and asking, "Who's come this way to give this woman to become the wife of this man?" Believe me when I tell you this: I answered it with a certainty and peace. *I do* was my inward reply to the unspoken question. And I did.

A sense of transfer happened as I laid hands on Chris and prayed. Maybe more intentionally and introspectively than any other time they had collectively gathered as a family, the congregation stepped from their seats as a personal declaration of intent. Cinderella was taking Prince Charming by the hand.

And pray I did. The heart of my prayer still remains my prayer for Chris: "God, let Chris feel the full weight of Crossroads: the care of her people and the demands of her ministries. Not that he be crushed by it, though for an instant he might wonder, but that he can feel the unmistakable resurrection power of Your Presence as You put Your shoulder under the load and lift the burden to a level of partnership that proves You are there."

As I prayed that Chris would feel the burden on his shoulders, I felt undeniable relief on mine. The transition was not just something that was happening with Chris and me, it was something that was happening between Chris and the Great Shepherd. Only God can take two and make them one in marriage. That same God was taking the Cinderella He had entrusted into my care and was handing her off to Prince Charming.

The daddy-daughter dance was over, and the prince took her by the hand.

TIME TO REFLECT

. . . .

1) Who will be in charge of setting the schedule and agenda of celebrating the outgoing leader's tenure? What do you hope happens at the parties?

2) If you are on the leadership team, what would you like the pastor's farewell to look like?

3) If you are the outgoing leader, what one message do you want to leave that will echo in the souls of the congregation after you're gone?

4) What is an appropriate gift that you could give as a leader to the congregation that would mark the moment and underscore a value of your ministry?

5) Based on your experience as a leader, what are the blessings you pray God grants to your successor and his family?

PART 3

LIVING

THE NEW DAY

CHAPTER 12

DISCOVERING AND HONORING YOUR NEW BOUNDARIES

> *"No" is a complete sentence.*
>
> – ANNE LAMOTT

Anne Lamott understands boundaries. Oprah Winfrey has used this quote so often that some people erroneously credit her as its author. But frankly, if it wasn't my mom who came up with it first, I'd be shocked! Mom was creative in working the word no into our conversations: No; No, period; No means no; What part of no do you not understand? All of them confirm Lamott's power of the word.

EXCHANGE YOUR TUXEDO FOR BIG BOY PANTS

I've started light, but this chapter demands vulnerability far beyond comfort, both mine in revealing, and yours in employing. The party is over, but like every shindig, there's some clean up to do. Oddly enough, you can't pronounce a transition healthy until some time has passed and you've established a new normal. Make no mistake, the season is new and you must establish a normal that is just as current. These final steps will test your maturity at the deepest levels.

It's time to talk about some of the new realities after the dance is over. You cannot afford to wait until after the handoff to have the conversation about boundaries.

An effective approach to this subject would be a team discussion of Robert Frost's "Mending Fences." Its ambiguity causes you to think more than formulate, and that's precisely what a healthy approach to boundaries demands. Frost writes about two different viewpoints of the merit of walls. The first viewpoint he identifies with the words, "Something there is that doesn't love a wall." This statement sums up the counter viewpoint: "Good fences make good neighbors."

Before your final exit, sit down with your team and your successor, and work through Frost's poem with the intent of generating relevant discussion. The questions Frost raises will help you more than you know on the far side of the transition.

I've known from what I reference as the second email (I'll explain that later) that new boundaries had to be addressed, but I assumed it could be approached from a lighthearted side to make the point. Writing this chapter helped me understand the importance, the emotion, and the complexity of establishing new boundaries.

I genuinely questioned myself about the source of this present, unexpected tenderness; and it brought me face to face with the culprit: It was me. It was that part of me that feels safest when in control, and this was the first question in the transition for which the answer was simply not mine to give, but to live. Frost exposed me: "Something there is that doesn't love a wall."

Whatever you do in getting to the point of the exit, how you deal with boundaries is pivotal to the quality of life you will experience with

Cinderella and her prince after you step away. I thought I'd covered the boundaries before my last day. The distance at which I (by my own decision) would settle was measurably greater by the end of the transition than I had anticipated throughout most of the process. There were plenty of people who wondered if I could let go, but I wasn't one of them. And to this day, I think I did.

What I didn't recognize in time is that setting boundaries isn't simply an issue of possession, but of position. It is a question of distance. When you step aside, how far do you go? Where is a good place for you to settle to safeguard your healthy relationship and your successor's unencumbered leadership in this realignment?

To be candid, I got my hands slapped when I crossed a line I wasn't sure existed. I'll tell you the story in a moment, but the truth is, I deserved it. I didn't just wander close to the neighbor's fence: I climbed over it. It wasn't a serious encroachment, but it was a line that could justify a fence in the eyes of any new property owners.

Wanting to help you enjoy the benefits of a healthy transition brought me face to face with the reality that you mustn't do what I did. Even without the experience, my counsel to anyone else would have been different from my choice.

THE SECOND EMAIL

Untamed ornery boyishness didn't spark my actions, and it wasn't the devil that made me do it. I made a calculated decision, and I miscalculated. It was what I've often referred to as *the second email*.

Chris' first email came from Las Vegas and invited me into the happy process that led to my healthy exit. His second email clarified that my exit was complete and a new day had officially ensued.

It was five weeks after the transition. The church decided to hold on to several hundred chairs from the old auditorium. Though they were of some age, they were high quality, and we frequently found uses for them in various circumstances. We also had to store them.

A major flood inundated our community. A local church lost all of its furniture in the deluge and sustained that loss with no flood insurance. The administrative pastor and my reassigned personal assistant suggested that we give this church all the chairs they needed to replace its loss.

That wasn't a decision that two good-hearted leaders could make independently. They needed consensus and permission. The email went out to the leadership team, including lay leaders — an email group to which I still belonged. I did not know whether it was by oversight, or design. I did know how this group functioned and the intent of such emails. To that point, I had used that level of email, plus SPS (our intra-church communication email) to keep me informed as to how to pray for Chris and Crossroads in those early critical days, a habit I continue every morning to this day.

I was at my computer when the email arrived. As I read it, I thought the gift was such a good idea that I wanted to applaud them for thinking about it, let alone doing it. As I banged out my response, I caught myself thinking, You're going to blow your cover if you respond. If they didn't know you were still on this group list, they sure will now. This may be your last one. I was more right than I actually expected.

I told you it was calculated. My original motivation was sincere, but I knew as I hit the send button that it would function as a trial balloon. I felt like a farm kid driven by curiosity to come even closer to an electric fence, knowing it could be hot, but not certain. Once you reach out and touch that wire, you don't have to wonder anymore. Well, that electric fence was hot and I discovered a new boundary.

The response wasn't crude, but it was clear. It wasn't what anyone said, but what no one said. I didn't hear a thing! I never saw a single reply from the other recipients. In fact, I never officially heard the final decision regarding the chairs. And what's more, I quit getting the SPS as well! I effectually entered the dark ages of Crossroads' news and information.

I knew exactly what happened. Someone confirmed it some months later. Before the second opinion of the group on the matter was expressed, a question regarding my continued presence on the leadership list was raised, coupled with an edict to change that fact immediately. Furthermore, the process of removing my name from that list inadvertently removed me from the SPS: a list on which I would rationally continue in light of my ongoing status as a small group leader. When I said communication went dark, it did. I heard nothing for months.

In the context of a catch-up conversation with my friend who originated the email to which I had replied, as well as effecting the removal of my name from the group, I broached the subject. Old habits die hard. I offered my conjecture of the sequence of events that triggered my unplugged status. With a smile, he confirmed Chris had a negative response to my vote of approval. Embarrassingly, my friend offered that the removal of my name from the leadership list triggered the deletion of my name from the SPS list. He had remained unaware of the extent of the deletion until our conversation.

It may have been hope against hope that hit the send instead of the delete button, but I could have avoided the awkwardness by my simply asking about the boundaries, rather than stumbling headlong across them. The response may have been extempore, but it wasn't unjust.

GETTING OFF THE FENCE ABOUT FENCES

The only purpose worth the risk of revealing this embarrassing moment is to spare you from one of your own. The thoughts it fosters, the awkwardness that results, and the pain it metes is no fun.

Whichever side of the fence you're on in Frost's poem, I was proof that good fences do make good neighbors. I got off the fence about the subject.

One of the few absolutes Frost settles is that these guys aren't on the same side of the fence in this matter of building walls: "Something there is that doesn't love a wall" being held by the one, and "Good fences make good neighbors" being adhered to by the other.

Let the poet take you to the mat with the tension of these two individuals. They were people who shared so much in common that they found themselves neighbors. Yet they were so different in their view of the effect of fences on their relationship that they had to learn to live with their differences as much as they did the wall itself.

I chuckle at the stanza about cows. The speaker in the poem finally concedes that there might well be some circumstances where fences could be helpful. He acknowledges there might be some holy cows in the field that warrant consideration in a discussion about fences.

I encourage you to engage each other in a discussion that addresses the health and vulnerabilities of your transition. We should have considered some holy cows for the benefit of Chris and the church before I left.

ENGINEERING GUIDELINES FOR A FENCE

So, if getting off the fence about fences finds you landing on the side that believes good fences make good neighbors, then you have to make some decisions about where to build them. We learned some lessons that might be helpful.

NO CRISIS SOLVING ALLOWED

When a woman leaves her daddy to become one with her prince, she must begin looking to her prince in tough times. That shift is also a necessary part of a healthy transition, though it is not always a natural one. There is but one exception to this rule for me, and that would be at the invitation of the successor. Chris can ask me advice for anything; he has an open door to me at any time. But it would be limited to exactly that: solicited advice.

For every iconic ministry that has suffered from the ill-advised intrusion of a former leader into issues that arose after his or her departure, others struggled under the radar with similar issues. The damage it inflicts on the Kingdom and the pain it imposes on the people who call it home are equivalent when measured at the personal level.

Cross only the throne room's threshold with your concerns and pray, pray, pray; but honor that same fence you appreciated when you were on the other side.

THE HONEYMOON

God buried Moses in an unmarked grave and let John the Baptist remain on death row until he was martyred. I'm not positive of the correlation between their circumstances and our subject, but these great leaders were both escorted out of the picture of their successor's first days of senior leadership. I do know fathers don't go on the honeymoon with the prince and princess.

I made a mistake in failing to let people know how long I believed Chris and Crossroads needed for the honeymoon period. It raised some questions, both about my level of comfort with Chris and my authenticity in caring for the people. I regret that, but the relationships were so healthy at my departure, and the exchanges were sufficient in the year to follow, that any concerns were alleviated.

After our exit, Becky and I spent most of the following few months traveling or visiting other churches. We waited nearly six months before we walked back through the doors the first time for a Sunday morning service, and even then we were very much under the radar. Though we continued to lead a small group and Becky helped at a minimal level in the children's ministry, we were not involved in any other ministries.

After the six months had elapsed, Becky and I began attending Crossroads more consistently, showing up at any one of the three weekend services about three times a month. We also continued to support them with our tithe. After the initial travel period I referenced earlier, we began attending a church about thirty miles away. We loved the pastor and his wife, and thoroughly enjoyed the worship and the pastor's preaching. In this current season, we have continued to slip into Crossroads when convenient (sounds like we've become casual churchgoers!), but attend our new church weekly. We were used to four services a weekend while pastoring, so going to two weekend services after our transition is no big deal!

If your circumstances allow for a choice to be made, I wouldn't return for any public worship service before six months. Six months felt comfortable as we walked through the doors for the first time back. I thought that if we waited any longer, it would create a different sort of awkwardness.

NO SECOND GUESSING

We've already talked about entering the fray of a crisis. The only difference between a crisis and second-guessing your successor's decision is that the latter will create the former. Don't do it. God has enough Monday morning quarterbacks, as well as godly counselors, to serve in the role of quality control. Neither God, nor our successor, needs another armchair quarterback.

INVITATIONS TO STAFF FUNCTIONS

Nine months after my departure, Becky and I received an invitation to the staff Christmas party. The planners consulted Chris before the invitation and we had a wonderful time, but I felt uncomfortable at times being there. They did anything but mistreat us. They paid too much attention to us. The experience confirmed in my heart what I feared before we went: It was their first Christmas together, and our presence felt like an intrusion. I was so grateful for the invite, but I think it would have been wiser to take a snow check until the following year.

TIMING IS EVERYTHING

Chris and I talked about my return to the platform before I left, and we've talked about it since. The operative word is "talked." I would presume nothing on your successor and stay sensitive to the circumstances. If the time comes that our successor believes we can be of value to Cinderella, not just to fill a weekend or meet our own personal need, then a return to the platform can work. I would feel comfortable with a plan to return to the platform after a year.

IN-HOUSE MINISTRY REQUESTS

At the request of the leadership team of Heaven's Hands, and with Chris' blessing, I was asked to speak at its dedication. Because this ministry targeted the whole community, members of the community were serving on the team, and leaders outside of Crossroads had played a key role in catalyzing its initiation, I felt at complete liberty to speak.

If not an obvious infringement on your successor's turf, filter any request to participate in church events or ministry roles through him.

SERVICE PERIMETER

I would never accept a call to serve as a leader within reasonable driving distance of your former church. Even the business world establishes non-competitive clauses in their transitions. You are undoubtedly as aware as I am of those kinds of breaches and you remember your gut response to the news whenever somebody crossed the line. Those infringements generally follow an unhealthy transition and almost always have an unhealthy impact.

Take the lead on this and don't put your successor in an uncomfortable position to set the standard. Develop a rule of thumb that you could live with if you were Prince Charming and your predecessor was staying in the community.

APPROPRIATE COMMUNICATION

I accept an invitation to chat with Chris any time he extends it. We are talking with increasing frequency, and I count these conversations as very enjoyable. Our talks have been exchanges with no restrictions or uneasiness. I look forward to continuing that dialogue.

I began having conversations with my longstanding administrative pastor eleven months after we left. Those times together are equally enjoyable and honoring conversations.

All other staff members are by invitation only — theirs! Outside of the appropriate thank you notes, I had no contact for several months. I never thought to ask Chris about his thoughts on contact with his staff, but I wish I had. I think you and your successor should make the whole staff aware of the guidelines before you leave.

MAINTAINING MINISTRIES

As previously mentioned, I continued leading a small group and Becky accepted invitations to play roles in our children's ministries. Only the senior pastor should initiate a position of any kind and be accepted by you just as carefully after personal conversation to confirm the soundness of the strategy.

WEEKEND WORSHIP INTERACTIONS

My love to mingle and the individual response to me served as a marker to the wisdom of my return. Frankly, I am who I am. Cinderella is still my little girl. Mingling is what I do. Walking back into Crossroads is like getting together with the kids for dinner or holidays. I love to see them. I care about how they are doing. And I enjoy talking to them. I did not return to Crossroads on a regular basis until I felt comfortable to mingle.

When you can accept being the grandpa instead of the dad, when you understand the boundaries of which we've already addressed, and when you've talked to your successor about the issue, then there is no problem interacting with the people with whom you have such a deep connection.

WEDDINGS AND FUNERALS

Your tradition or established policy may already have set this boundary for you, but let me assure you it gets blurry with extended families and members of families with whom you've been connected for generations. Chris and I came to an early agreement that I would have the freedom to say yes to ceremonies involving families and individuals of longstanding relationships.

Outside of that, my new fence gives me unmitigated permission to say no. Cinderella's needs had commandeered my schedule for decades; that had to change. And it did. I have said no more than yes (to Becky's absolute joy)!

COUNSELLING POLICY

Cease and desist all counseling. Where lines might feel blurred, simply point the person toward your successor and his approach to counseling. I was so glad that the counseling load had long since been shared by the connected staff members and that Crossroads' culture was to meet the need, not dictate who had to meet it. It was an easy shift to step out of counseling almost altogether.

I had one situation that was so delicate and long-standing that I saw it through to a semblance of conclusion. I maintained friendships after I left which gave rise to circumstances wherein I counseled as their friend, not pastor. In this case, I believed the cow was more mine to guard than Crossroads' to determine.

SUPPORT THE NEW PRINCE

It can't be better said than Bob Russell in his book, *Transition Plan*. Some leaders find it difficult to move out of the spotlight. I understand why. After I had been gone for a couple of years I returned one Sunday to visit and one man who saw me in the restroom said, 'Hey, Bill! Good to see you back!' In two years he had forgotten my name. That's a huge blow to the ego. But at some point you have to go from being "the man" to "the biggest fan."

I don't have to work at this, but I keep telling people I'm the happiest I've ever been. Then I tell people that a primary reason I am is because I feel so good about the way Chris is leading and the increasing effectiveness of the church. I celebrate new programming and expanding membership as I talk about my departure from pastoring.

My grandpa was a real force in my spiritual development and the shaping of my worldview. He was one of the great storytellers in my childhood. Every time he slipped into the back seat of our family's car, or my brother and I walked with him through the fields doing some mundane task together, we asked him to tell us a story. Sometimes they were snippets of family history, and sometimes they were stories with a moral to weave into the fabric of his grandsons' souls.

Rarely did Grandpa surprise me with the moral to a story. In one such instance, he quoted Frost's "Mending Fences" as my brother and I were mending farm fences with him.

Being the admiring grandson, I always thought that whatever grandpa said was right. I had heard enough of his stories to get a basic handle on his guidelines to good manners and gracious responses to others. When I heard him quote Frost's work, I thought that the right answer to the role of fences with neighbors is to have no fences that separate you from them. He shocked me when he made it clear that he thought it took good fences to keep a good neighbor! Experience has brought me to the conclusion that Grandpa was right.

TIME TO REFLECT

· ·

1) On which side of the fence do you land when thinking about the need for boundaries? Do fences ever make good neighbors? When?

2) What is your natural response to boundaries you didn't establish?

3) What are the natural forces that put pressure on thoughtful boundaries?

4) What would be included on the list of healthy boundaries to provide a working margin for your successor?

5) What is a healthy response to a breach of either side of the line?

CHAPTER 13

THE UNFINISHED ROCKS

> *Summing it all up, friends, I'd say*
> *you'll do best by filling your minds*
> *and meditating on things true, noble,*
> *reputable, authentic, compelling,*
> *gracious — the best, not the worst;*
> *the beautiful, not the ugly;*
> *things to praise, not things to curse.*
>
> – PHILIPPIANS 4:8
> (THE MESSAGE)

Unless you're long past the time you should have left, the vision that energized your actions will not diminish on the same timetable that your exit plan is finished.

We've talked about one facet of that reality in the chapter detailing Heaven's Hands. But you have to face it: Try as you might, there are some things you're just not going to accomplish, and you have to be prepared to wait, at best, for someone else to do them. And you'll save yourself some consternation if you prepare for them to not be accomplished at all.

The point of this chapter is to help you prepare for the reality that some of your unfinished projects could become an irritant later.

DOING WHAT'S NATURAL

Vision really does drive a leader. I believe values drive your vision. Experience confirms what Jesus said: "For where your treasure is, there your heart will be also" (Matthew 6:21). You find yourself thinking about what's most important to the point that it's the last thing you think about before you go to sleep and the first thing on your mind after you wake up.

Vision has been easy for me. As a leader, God has given me the capacity to focus on my values to the point that it produces an image in my mind that has some detail to it. Something inside compels me to take what I have and turn it into something I want. And that's a character trait I just can't turn off. My visionary urges probably had me hitting the accelerator instead of the break as I approached the last days of my tenure.

It's easy to understand how overdriving is a vulnerability of leaders. Lists do not drive leaders; they drive managers. Leaders are driven by what creates the list — bottlenecks and constrictions; what's missing or messed up; the next step to get you where you're going or being who you're becoming. Leaders' eyes don't drift; their hearts direct their feet. If you can find out what a leader is looking at, you can tell where his or her heart is.

Every list of leadership quotes includes Steven Covey's leadership axiom: "Management works in the system; leadership works on the system." As leaders, we suspect the system could always use a little work.

After I see what my heart says to do, then I start looking for what is out of alignment or a point of obstruction in the picture. That becomes a game plan for coordinating actions to get reality aligned with possibility. That is a convoluted way of saying I'm a critic. I'm a critic with an eye toward progress, not a judge looking to berate a person or simply rate a finished product. But I'm a critic, nonetheless. And that always keeps me at least a little unsettled; and sometimes it can cheat me out of enjoying the beauty of what is. It did that after I stepped down from pastoring Crossroads.

A PEBBLE IN YOUR SHOE

I get a reminder of my critical nature every time I drive down one of Crossroads' drives. It's my own fault: I put the reminders there. They are like pebbles in my shoe, and they started rubbing me raw within a few weeks of Cinderella's and Prince Charming's wedding.

I spent three very cold days in February before my exit in March securing one last pile of big rocks. I'm talking boulders. These rocks were so big that if they talked they would have deep voices. Since Jesus said something awesome about rocks crying out (Luke 19:40), I believe you can use rocks to send a message. I believed that strategically placed rocks along our drive would cry out to every person who leaves the campus as a reminder of the principles they couldn't afford to forget after they got home.

With the help of a friend and some large equipment, I positioned the rocks in what I believed would maximize their visibility. My plan was to inscribe the boulders with the mantras of Crossroads; slogans developed to drive home core values.

Before I finished, it became obvious that we were not going to get the job done before I was gone. I made a calculated decision to take the project as far as my time allowed, and that the barefaced rocks would serve as secondary messages to remind leadership to complete the project. I assumed that condition would be temporary.

Well, what I believed to be temporary may turn out to be permanent. All the rocks remain blank to this day. What I had hoped would be a prod to them after I was gone, became a goad to me each time I went back.

LEARNING NOT TO STARE

When my parents' pastor in Florida was asked how he felt about guys wearing earrings, he gave an answer that was based on a principle I needed to hear. The pastor told the person digging for a controversial answer that he had just gained new perspective on the issue. He identified a young guy they both highly regarded, then added the detail of a recently acquired earring by the young disciple. The earring was initially an accessory you couldn't help but notice. The pastor had no question of the kid's love for Jesus and his faithfulness in living it out. His answer to the question in light of this kid was, "I just learned not to stare at it."

The fact he was a high-ranking, retired military officer, as well as the pastor of a large, fundamentalist church stereotyped him in my mind. I didn't think he had it in him to overlook what was irritating. But I was wrong. He understood Philippians 4:8 and made one of the most practical applications of it I've ever heard. His military experience had prepared him for the reality that there are hills to die on, and earrings aren't one of them. And it's the perfect response to any blank rocks I pass along the church drive.

So, what do you do? I can tell you quickly what not to do: Don't stare at them. Paul's advice to the Philippians really does nail this one: " . . . (fill) your minds and (meditate) on things true, noble, reputable, authentic, compelling, gracious — the best, not the worst; the beautiful, not the ugly; things to praise, not things to curse" (Philippians 4:8, THE MESSAGE).

A PRESCRIPTION FOR RELIEF

WHAT *IS* RATHER THAN WHAT *ISN'T*

Typically, I look at what isn't, so I can figure out a way that it can be. Not staring at earrings for that pastor was a conscious decision. It had to become a conscious decision for me not to stare at the rocks.

So many great things are going on at Crossroads. Scores of people have trusted Christ. Growing numbers of people understand God's role in their finances. The number of people I don't know increases at every service I attend. The list goes on ad infinitum. I would have to overlook so much to fixate on those rocks.

Try looking and listening for the kinds of things that made Paul's list in Philippians and develop one of your own. You can't just tell your mind what not to think; you have to direct it onto something healthier. You can't just close your eyes; you have to redirect them.

REMEMBER THE VISION

You didn't hire a curator. So, expect strategies and programming to adjust, maybe even change considerably over time. If your successor is aligned with the mission and vision of the church, then he will understand what you wanted to accomplish, not just how to mimic what you did. When you see all the effort and resources being expended on mission-critical steps, then be grateful those efforts aren't dissimilar at their core. Freshness in approach can add new dimensions to the achievement of the same goal.

BE PATIENT

Forget timetables. You're off the clock. Pray for your successor's success, but let God decide the cycles and set the rhythms.

James' words are what we need to hear when we start to get edgy about the church we love: "But let patience have its perfect work, that you may be perfect and complete, lacking nothing" (James 1:4).

The Italians have turned this scripture's application into a proverb: "One minute of patience can result in ten years of peace." Having patience and peace help you keep a good relationship with your successor and both are essential to the church's well-being.

Vegas pays attention to any edge that changes the odds and so should we. W.B. Prescott was quoted as saying, "In any contest between power and patience, bet on patience." You're much better off to be patient when it comes to unfinished rocks, rather than to start throwing stones.

MEASURING PROGRESS

The Lord prepared me before I stepped away from Crossroads that we would be addressing the paradox of my life. I had led a church for thirty-eight years through weekend worship and personally failed at remembering the Sabbath. The Voice that had become so familiar in helping me help others let me know I wasn't good at remembering the Sabbath because I didn't understand the heart of Sabbath. That was going to change.

Oh, I worshipped. And I understood at a reasonably high-level worship's possibilities and power, but I missed the essential element of resting on the Sabbath. Rest and Sabbath find their base in the same basic Hebrew words. And the fourth commandment says to remember it.

The first time resting shows up in Scripture is in the blueprints of our world, and it is God who rests. He wasn't tired, but He did rest. So what in the world could that mean?

Rabbi Berel Wein's remarks in his article "The Power of

Remembering" are once again notable to this point. He says, in part:

> "One of the basic requirements of Judaism is the gift of memory ... Memory is the most essential trait for Jewish continuity and success ... Memory always needs positive reinforcement to be preserved and treasured."

So, God spent the seventh day thinking about how creation came together and hearing the angels sing in absolute awe as it did. I believe God stopped to muse on how far His world had come and then celebrated it.

God designed us to remember and then told us to do it by enjoying the moments the journey had provided to date. He knew that when we remember what has happened, it will always lead us to Him; and in that spirit of awe, we would worship. We just get too busy with what is left undone to consider what has been done.

I think that is why this has been the happiest season of my life. I'm learning to celebrate where I am and how I got here, not where I'm going and how to get there. I'm taking the time to enjoy the now by honoring the time that led up to it, not jumping into tomorrow before it gets here. Maybe the first message God wanted those rocks along the drive at Crossroads to cry out was for me; maybe I needed to hear a message from unfinished stones, rather than feel frustration by the lack of inscriptions.

Decide now to celebrate what has happened and is happening with your Cinderella and her Prince Charming. Quit worrying about what yet needs to happen. Doing this will turn your worry into worship. After all, God released you from the responsibility when He said you were finished with your part. Now rest and let remembering refresh you during the seventh day.

FAN THE FLAME DIFFERENTLY

Becky has never had to wake me during a service led by someone else, but she has given me some well-placed and well-timed jabs. Not long after we returned to Crossroads, Becky had a challenging conversation with me. I'm a nail-biter — a horrible habit, I admit. Becky knows my triggers. After a couple of services, she confronted me. "Quit biting your nails, sit up, and lean forward. People are watching you and assessing your actions. I hope Chris doesn't see you; he'll think it's because of him."

No wonder God said it is not good for a man to be alone (Genesis 2:18). It embarrassed and shamed me to think I could have sent any kind of negative vibes to or about Chris. He deserved better, and I should have done better. It had nothing to do with Chris, but more to do with learning how to relax when you've got nothing to do with what's happening.

I had continued to pray for Chris and Crossroads every morning during my devotional time, but I determined then that I would tell him. I have made it a point to find times to verbalize it. I also shoot him an email or text to celebrate what's happening or remind him that I'm praying.

If anyone understands all the demands of taking care of Cinderella, you do. If anyone knows the impact of hard winters or long athletic seasons on the stats and continuity of the church, you do. So, if anyone should be able to recognize the pressures that preempt rock inscribing, you should. Just keep driving.

NURTURING MUTUAL RESPECT

The best way to nurture mutual respect is to spend time with the other person. It doesn't have to crowd a schedule, and it doesn't have to be a conversation to catch up on all the news. Let it be time around the table that reminds you that he's still a real person, with a real family, and real demands, who may do occasionally what you did: cry in the shower or find a dark auditorium where you can let it all out. You know the load he's carrying. Just spend some time with your successor.

You might still be carrying the load your successor is carrying had he not agreed to take it for you. And he may need to be reminded from time to time that you were right in choosing him as your successor. You believed it then, so tell him again how right you were. That will rekindle your love if it's waned, and nurture mutual respect.

LET IT GO

Live with the fact you took both the rocks and the vision as far as you could take them, and you did it to the last day you had to take them there.

If God wants those rocks inscribed, He will make sure it happens. God is going nowhere. You're done. He's not. If they were His rocks in the beginning, they are still His now. And your successor may or may not like the rocks as much as you do, but he has ears, too. God knows how to use them. So, let it go.

TIME TO REFLECT

. . . .

1) As a leader, how do you deal with letting go?

2) What are the internal indicators you can use to monitor as a forewarning

of the development of unhealthy attitudes after you complete the transition?

3) What is the most meaningful way you can communicate encouragement to your successor?

4) What could be the advantages of an ongoing dialogue between the outgoing leader and the successor after the transition?

5) What could you envision as a healthy schedule for setting such interactions?

CHAPTER 14

. . . .

FINISHED

| *It is finished.*

> – JESUS
> (JOHN 19:30)

The concept "It is finished" was not first introduced from the Cross. The first time we hear those words is the record of God's assessment of His work in creation. In the Pentateuch, Moses records the milestone of the end of creation, "By the seventh day God had finished the work he had been doing" (Genesis 2:2).

According to John 1:1-3, not only was Jesus present at creation, but it also all happened through Him. Then, after work on Friday night, He sat back for a season and enjoyed what He had created. Jesus obviously was not finished with everything, let alone our world, but He was finished with that phase of His plan. So, He was perfectly familiar with the word before He used it from the cross.

In fact, He did exactly the same thing after He got back to heaven from His mission on earth by way of the tomb. Again, God felt it important for us to know what Jesus did after He was finished: He sat down at the right hand of the Father until … (see Hebrews 1:3, 13).

Until. It's interesting to think about God choosing the exact word to detail a circumstance or convey a thought (and He always does). Since we are talking about the end of our tenure and the transition of leadership and, more importantly, realizing Cinderella has always been His baby and we were playing the role He assigned, then using His word to describe our status is insightful: *finished.*

Branson, Missouri, became the Monday morning destination after our Sunday goodbye at Crossroads. We went to unwind and reflect for a couple of weeks. Branson worked. When the first Sunday morning came, we went to visit Ted Cunningham at Woodland Hills Church in Branson. He had been at Crossroads a few months before, and we had talked about connecting, so we did. After services, he became the first person to ask me, "So, Jeff, how do you feel?"

I hadn't taken time to formulate an answer, let alone get one in the can, so it was off the cuff and in the rough. After a pause long enough for the word to come to mind, I said it for the first time: "Finished. I feel finished, Ted. I don't feel burned out or washed up. I'm running from nothing and ready for whatever, but in playing my role at Crossroads, I'm finished."

Maybe I'm the only preacher with this problem, but it's easier to finish my tenure than it is to finish my answer to a question, so it continued with an analogy that popped into my mind.

Jesus didn't leave His post one second before He was finished with what He came to do, but you can rest assured that He didn't stay one second longer than it took to atone sufficiently for every sin — and that by the Father's standards. Jesus truly did pay for it all — every sin for every person. He had experienced all the shame and felt all the pain caused by every sin. He had taken the worst humanity can dole out. He suffered the ridicule of every demon of hell. It had all run its horrible course, and He crossed the finish line. It was over. He had done it, and He was *finished!*

I made reference of this fact to Ted. But it was not the last time I would think about Ted's question, my answer, and Jesus' use of that word.

My purpose for writing this book is not simply to give you a formula or to get my experience in print. I want to help you give your Cinderella the best opportunity to succeed beyond your leadership. To ensure that the prince and princess do not lose a step as they continue to pursue the mission to which Jesus, the real Prince Charming, has called them.

I want to help you experience the joy of my first breath and how I expended it.

I want you to take your first step with the greatest blessing anyone can experience, especially one that's been mapped by the God of the Universe and the Head of the church. I want you to experience the total release and freedom of being finished. It's a foretaste of what we have to look forward to in heaven.

There were some unexpected surprises as the daddy-daughter dance ended on my final Sunday at Crossroads. I want you to know what they were, because I am certain they are not reserved just for me.

A HINT OF HEAVEN

It was as rewarding for me as it will be for you to hear people we love and respect say, "Thank you for . . ." or "You're the best." But it was an unanticipated moment to sense the Great Shepherd say, "Good job, Jeff. Thank you for taking care of My sheep."

We all want to hear, "Good job. I'm proud of you" when we stand before Jesus, but I wasn't dead yet! This wasn't an event or a weekend that was over; this was my role at Crossroads. While I was inhaling my first breath as the church's former senior pastor, and not my last breath as the former everything I had ever been, the Lord wanted me to know that not only was the job done, but also, just as He had pronounced over creation on a Friday night, "It is good; in fact, it is very good."

I will never forget that kiss of approval from the Father on this little boy's head.

It is my highest hope that you will get the same privilege as you walk off the stage, whether it's the auditorium platform or the limelight of a public position. You really can anticipate that the Lord will have an opinion of what you've done and a willingness to express it. You've read them, but there's coming a moment you'll get to experience the words written by the author of Hebrews: "For God is not unjust. He will not forget how hard you have worked for him and how you have shown your love to him by caring for other believers . . ." (Hebrews 6:10, NLT).

The last memorial video had been played. The last card had been placed in our hands. The last gift had been given. And my blessing prayer over Chris had been prayed. When I said "amen," it was over: not my love for Crossroads, nor their love for me. Not our mutual hopes for God's best in the future, but our relationship as we had experienced it. After nearly thirty-eight years, I was not their pastor anymore. The privilege of leading them into the future was not my assignment anymore. And I knew it. All the way to the bottom of my heart, I knew it. I had finished what God had asked.

On a late night fifteen years earlier, He made sure I heard the ticking clock so I could be preparing for this: "I've been thinking about this a lot longer than you have. You didn't start it and you won't finish it. You have a role to play in the process of it." That message came early enough to get my heart acclimated to the reality and my eyes open for my successor.

The plan He had devised for a great church, long before I ever gave it a thought, was not finished. The follow through of His plan that had commenced before me and would continue after me, was not finished, but the role I was to play in it was finished.

The extension of His love for our community through Crossroads was not finished, but my casting of the vision for it was finished.

It was the strangest and yet sweetest feeling of my life. It really was a hint of heaven.

WHAT IS "FINISHED" ANYWAY?

I will never forget sitting in the locker room of the gymnasium of Frankfort High School as a freshman. We had just lost the championship game of our sectional in the Indiana High School Basketball Tournament. I was disappointed, but then again, I was a freshman. The seniors were done and their emotions were deeper than mine. It was the oddest thing for a fourteen-year-old kid to be thinking, but I did a quick mental calculation to help me deal with the end of the season: Even if we were to lose the first game of my three remaining sectionals, I have sixty-three more games to play.

As it turned out, I had sixty-six games on my schedule, but as sure as I had found myself on that bench my freshman year, I found myself back on that same bench sixty-six games later. I can't believe it, I said to myself. I sat right here sixty-six games ago with all of them ahead of me. They are over. They are all over. It didn't feel the same as a senior as it did as a freshman — because it wasn't. It was over.

It comes to that for us, you know.

The wedding days for Leslie, Jessica, and Jennifer came and went. Like their mother before them, they each walked the aisle as the most beautiful brides I have ever seen. But they were different from their mother because they were walking with me, not to me. The moment I answered the question the pastor asked me, Becky and I both felt the official completion of the transition. Please don't misunderstand; I assure you that our repurposed role is a happy one. When our daughters call asking for input as they raise their own family, we feel honored. Being grandparents to their kids is as fun and rewarding as it was having them on our heels or cheering for them from the stands when they were kids. But it was undeniable: the guardian nature of our relationship as mom and dad was over.

It comes to that for us, you know.

The last wedding, the last funeral, the last counseling session, the last meeting, the last service, the last message; it comes and goes. And then it is over.

It comes to that for us, you know.

But of all those lasts, the Lord made sure no other compared to my last Sunday at Crossroads. My basketball career never measured up to my dreams, while my girls continue to exceed my highest expectations. Though my tenure as pastor included some heartache, it was mostly an experience of grateful awe. As I stepped back from the crowd, walked off the platform, and finally out the door, I felt the warmth of God's presence. Jesus was right there. At the beginning of my pastoring career, He had asked me to do it, and at the beginning of the transition process, He had been first to inform me who was officially going to replace me.

Both times He was right there to convey a message He would not trust to another. That didn't change on my last day as the pastor around noon at the bottom of the steps of the Crossroads platform. He had never been closer. And He never will be closer to you.

FINISHED DOESN'T MEAN OVER

Two things were not over.

The first began almost as quickly as I said "amen" on my final morning at Crossroads. I had nothing to do with planning the services that weekend, so I didn't know how the service was supposed to end. But as our worship leader and team assembled on the stage for a closing song, I knew it wasn't just amen, high-fives, and we're out of here.

Right then and there, it hit me. Just as the Spirit had asked me what I shared with you at the beginning of this book, "Do you know where you are?" I was sensing that the coordinates of my journey were marking a special spot in time and experience. I knew exactly what I wanted to do.

That corner God had pointed out some fifteen years earlier when He revealed the vision of a place of hope and redemption for the sick and tired: We were right there. That hill He had sanctified and reserved for His own purposes in north central Indiana, even before the first man took his first step on the planet: We were right there, worshipping the very One that so deserved our adoration.

God's original call was for us to move the facilities to this particular hill, at this busiest of crossroads in north central Indiana, within sight of thousands going down roads they didn't want to travel, and ending up in places they didn't want to be. Remember His instructions? "I want you to give them an option."

I had known within a few ticks of the clock that night when the light turned red that the start of God's new plan for Crossroads had turned green. I began taking steps to accomplish what He wanted, and where He wanted it to happen. I was experiencing the last breaths of my tenure, and I was right there on the very spot He had revealed.

We had entered into a partnership with heaven itself and we had done it. More than getting closer to people, more than giving them options, right there, on the hill He had pointed out, people had made life-changing, eternity-impacting choices — just like He had wanted, just like He had promised. Some fifteen years later, I had lived the dream and experienced a church that morphed into a real force for the Kingdom.

The style with which we worshiped was the result of a directive some thirty years earlier. I had wondered if these people I loved and this place I served were right. I had adjusted some theological viewpoints and it wasn't in full alignment with our tradition. In a moment of my internal quandary, the Spirit made it clear that He needed a worshiping church where He could bring people from both ends of the Christian worship style continuum to meet and make them one. To put it in the terms of my dear mentor, Jack Hayford, "Worship isn't the end of everything, but it is the fountainhead of everything." We would be a worshiping church. What I had sensed as the call in that now distant moment was exactly what we were doing in this precious, present moment of transition.

My call was to pastor. It included preaching, but it was a call to more than that. Becky had shared in the call in the same week I received mine. We were both oblivious to the gentle whisper the other was hearing, but as I shared my call to pastor, Becky broke into tears with her short, but clear directive from God: "Be strong; you're going to be a pastor's wife." Though I had left heel marks in the road at seasons of my life, I often said to the people of Crossroads, "I didn't know He was talking about you, and about this, when He asked me to pastor." The scale of it would have scared me, but the who He gave me to pastor would have wooed me. And here they were: the people I didn't know then, but He did.

In that moment, it came together. I had been honored for doing something I didn't choose, for people I didn't previously know, on a hill that had looked more like a cornfield, and with worship that was a shift from my tradition. God seemed to be celebrating as much in that precious moment as the people were. And it broke me. In that brokenness, I knew with all my heart exactly what I wanted to do.

FROM MY HEART TO YOURS

What I'm about to share with you I wrote in a letter of gratitude to the people of Crossroads. There's no reason to say it differently, because I want you to know what I wanted those precious people to know. Here is an excerpt of my last letter to Crossroads:

The last of my thanks is for something of which you might never know, but the most precious of all to me. I want you to know what it is and why I'm so grateful. The Holy Spirit had already put it in words through the experience of David in Psalm 118. Not by chance, but by sequence I came to that psalm for my devotions the morning after we arrived at South Mineral Campground in the San Juan Mountains of Colorado.

It was the first thing I heard from The Voice, and it included you. I told you that this campground has been a sweet spot of connection for the Lord and me for forty years. The first time was shortly after I knew God had called me to a ministry that would shape every future decision of my life. It was one of the early places of singing the song of my life to Him.

While studying Psalm 118, I came to realize it ended with the same words with which it started. Both verses 1 and 29 say, "Give thanks to the LORD, for He is good; His love endures forever."

I enjoyed a God-moment in being reminded of the full circle I was completing. I felt exactly, what Spurgeon believed David was expressing in that Psalm: "You can bet the farm (or something like that) that the notes at the close of the loud hallelujah were more swift, more sweet, more loud than at the beginning." David started the song, but quickly began to invite others to sing with him. The rest of the psalm supplies the words and reasons to sing that powerful chorus. And over the course of his life, others did, in fact, join him, including all of us as we read what he wrote and make those words an expression of our own hearts.

I read those words and knew that I was singing the same song today as I was as a seventeen-year-old, knowing I had been called to ministry, not having a clue what all that would mean. I would have kicked less had I known the people who would join my little, private song of worship I was singing as an untested pastor. One of the joys of this season is thinking about those people who are now singing that song with me, making it sweeter, louder, and stronger today than it was when I sang alone. It felt like Sunday on a Thursday morning.

At the conclusion of my last service at Crossroads, the reins already in the hands of Chris, the blessing prayers already prayed, I felt the full weight of my responsibility lift and a sense of finishing what He had called me to do. And what He had described was fulfilled in that moment as you gathered together over the course of three services that weekend.

It was a crowning moment, but not the highest. That came as I experienced a foretaste of heaven when Jeff Hart led us and you joined him in singing what has become the worship song of my life. That little chorus gave us the words to sing as we declared our love for the Lord and sang of the joy He had given to us. You and I implored our King to hear our song of worship, and hoped with all of our heart that our words would be a sweet sound in His ears.

I asked you to worship and allow me a moment to listen. As I turned from you and before Him, I realized you were giving me the greatest gift. In that precious moment, you gave me the fulfillment of my calling to offer back to the One who asked me to do this. I knew in that moment what Revelation 4:10 describes as the elders gathered around the throne and laid their crowns at the feet of God. Like David with Israel, over the years of walking with the Lord, you had joined with me in my worship. It was the same song, but with more energy and beauty than when I sang alone. It was one of the most intimate moments of my life. Thank you.

THE STORY OF THE FORK

The second thing that is not over is your relationship with the Father and your place in His plan.

Only a dad knows what it's like to say, "I do" to a pastor with his Cinderella on his arm and Prince Charming at his side. But that lump in the throat gives way to a new reality. No more insurance bills for teens or tuition bills for career-minded kids. It's all replaced with a great daughter-in-law who loves my son, and sons-in-law who love my daughters, as well as the coolest thing in the world — thirteen grandkids! I'm telling you, I didn't know what "I do" really meant, or I would've been dancing down the aisle, instead of waiting until after the ceremony to dance!

It's a healthy transition we're talking about here, not an escort out the door. Six days of hard work and happy successes finally come to an end. The seventh day of rest and reflection will come and go (it did for God in Genesis). And the eighth day? Well, you know, it came, too.

Mine hasn't just yet. I'm still enjoying the weekend, but I'm sure it will.

And the fork thing? In case you've never heard the story:

A woman was diagnosed with a terminal illness and given three months to live. She asked her pastor to come to her home to discuss her final wishes. She told him which songs she wanted sung at her funeral, and what scriptures she wanted read, and which outfit she wanted to be buried in.

Then she said, "One more thing ... I want to be buried with a fork in my hand."

The pastor was surprised.

The woman explained, "In all my years of attending church socials and potluck dinners, I always remember that when the dishes of the main course were being cleared, someone would inevitably say to everyone, 'Keep your fork.' It was my favorite time of the dinner, because I knew something better was coming, like velvety chocolate cake or deep-dish apple pie — something wonderful. So, I want people to see me there in that casket with a fork in my hand and wonder, 'What's with the fork?' Then, I want you to tell them, 'Keep your fork, because the best is yet to come.'"

YOUR NEW BEGINNING

The end of our tenure is not the end. The daddy-daughter dance is over, and Cinderella and the prince are doing a dance of their own; the transition is completed, but just like the fairytale, our story is not over. It is a new beginning, and it has started with what has been the happiest year of my life.

I've written this book with the deepest certainty and the highest hope that it will be for you, too. Keep your fork, because after you and Cinderella are finished dancing…you get to eat the cake, too!

TIME TO REFLECT

. . . .

1) What do you envision "finished" looking like when your transition is completed?

2) What are the objectives God used you to help Him bring to reality during your tenure?

3) What do you want other people to say when they repeat the story of your leadership transition?

4) What do you look forward to most in celebrating your seventh day?

5) Do you believe that God has an eighth day for you? What do you think it might look like?

ABOUT THE AUTHOR

Jeff Harlow pastored Crossroads Community Church in Kokomo, Indiana for nearly 38 years.

Crossroads grew from less than 60 to a congregation of more than 3,000. The scope of the church's mission expanded from serving a handful of families to reaching thousands across north central Indiana. He led Crossroads through a strategic succession plan that ended with the reigns of leadership in Chris Duncan's hands and the church in full stride in its mission. He and Becky, his wife of 42 years, are the parents of 4 children and have 13 grandchildren.

You can reach Jeff at jeffharlow@ecrossroads.org or leave him a voicemail at 1-(765)-450-9678. Keep up with his latest projects by visiting www.epiphanypublishing.us/jeffharlow.

ABOUT THE PUBLISHER

Epiphany Publishing, LLC is a private publishing company based in Indianapolis, IN. We are devoted to exploring catalysts for growth in the fields of religion, psychology, business, and human development.

Each year, Epiphany Publishing donates 25% of all its profits to nonprofit organizations that fight profound injustice – especially those atrocities that rob the innocent of their future. This includes the global sex trade, child soldiers forced to fight in war, and other forms of unthinkable oppression. We invite you to join us in partnering with luminous, restorative organizations like saribari.com, warchild.org, worldvision.org, and antislavery.org.

We are always interested in meeting new authors and reviewing promising manuscripts. If you've got a transformational message that you believe would be a good fit to publish with us, please introduce yourself at www.epiphanypublishing.us.

EPIPHANY
PUBLISHING